C. E. Society
Presbyterian
Church
Olathe, Kans.

NEXT STEPS

AN ADVANCED TEXT-BOOK IN CHRISTIAN ENDEAVOR

BY

REV. W. F. McCAULEY,

Author of "How," "Why," Etc.

———

UNITED SOCIETY OF CHRISTIAN ENDEAVOR
BOSTON   CHICAGO

Plimpton Press

Printers and Binders, Norwood, Mass.

U. S. A.

TABLE OF CONTENTS.

PART I. AN ANALYTICAL STUDY.

PART II. SPECIAL FEATURES.

PART III. METHODS.

NEXT STEPS IN ENDEAVOR.

PART I.—An Analytical Study.

CHAPTER I.

THE ENDEAVOR MISSION.

It has been said that if the Society of Christian Endeavor did not shortly ally itself with some great cause, it would perish. Such a statement reveals profound and inexcusable ignorance of the principles of the movement. The Society *is* allied to a great cause—"For Christ and the Church." If it needs to champion some unique line of effort to exist, the sooner it gathers up its feet into its bed and dies in peace, the better. There have been enough special enterprises, or sorties out of the main body against this or that evil, or for the promotion of this or that interest; and there is need of a movement along the whole line. Our next step should be straight forward, with no turns or retrogressions to seek an easy path.

1. *The mission of any organization is to transfer its power into a permanent possession of the cause it propagates*, so that when the outward form

of its agency ceases, its spirit will still remain.
The Saviour made his physical presence unnec-
essary by sending the Spirit to teach the disciples "all things." The mission of any individual is so to labor that he will not be needed
after his death. On the tomb of the Wesleys are
these words: "God buries the worker, but carries
on the work." The Wesleys are no longer needed;
they made *themselves* useless by so laboring in the
fear of God that their work could go on without
them.

An orator, descanting upon the merits of Jabez
Bunting, a great apostle of Methodism, said,
"When Jabez Bunting died, the sun of Methodism set"; but a brother in the audience called
out, "Glory to God! That is a lie!" Methodism
no longer needs Jabez Bunting; he made *himself*
useless.

He is the truest Endeavorer who consciously
toils for "Christ and the church," that the
church may speedily become all and more than
he has helped to make his society. The society
is an expedient, in God's providence; as soon as
it becomes an end in itself, it has forgotten its
mission.

The heroes of faith, whose deeds are recorded
in the eleventh chapter of Hebrews, live over
again in the hearts of those their example in-
spired. They could afford to suffer and die to
give such immortality to the cause they loved.
No one need be jealous for his standing with the
future who serves God with full abandon now.
The possession of a present purpose to spend and

be spent for God is necessary to the proper fulfilment of any mission.

The Endeavor Society will accomplish its full tale of usefulness by carrying out to its logical sequence the motto it bears, "For Christ and the Church." Its effort should be to exalt the church in the world, to promote its efficiency, to labor for its thorough organization, till it is the most complete of all agencies, the most systematic, the most successful in emphasizing the individual obligation of its members and in training them for service.

2. *The mission of the Christian Endeavor movement is thus to spend its very life for the church.*—On that account, it is entitled to earnest support. It is a living thing, and seems to hear over again the exhortation of the beloved disciple, addressed to the young men because they were "strong." To transmute itself into an immortal force in the church, it must throb with activity and employ every opportunity for service; it must also receive the hearty support of Christians generally; and Endeavorers must practise avoidance of the numerous side-tracks which industrious evil lays for the ruin of the cause.

"What is the next step for Christian Endeavor?" we ask; and, like a child whose increasing self-consciousness and clearness of mental vision enable him to grasp the purpose of life, so the Endeavor movement, grown old enough to comprehend itself and its duty, responds, "The next step is to follow with concentration of purpose the single idea of giving to the church all I have and am." We may not know what God designs for the future. No one can be a prophet respecting the precise outcome of present movements any more than he can prophesy concerning his own future career; but sometime the grand result for which we have striven will be realized—the church made fully useful.

CHAPTER II.

That we may better understand the required step forward, let us glance at the past. We should not be enthusiasts, but take a just view of facts. There are persons who can make vigorous addresses, and who manifest an enthusiasm in speech that augurs great things, yet are found wanting in patient effort. Making allowance for individual effervescence and for unconscious exaggerations due to imperfect analysis, we must agree that the past achievements have been marvellous. They are of three classes: Personal piety, systematic work, and fellowship. These may be sufficiently illustrated by the last named.

1. *There has been an advance in interdenominational fellowship.*—Nor has this been at the expense of loyalty to the individual congregation. An unprejudiced view of the situation compels this conclusion, and whatever may seem to contradict is illusive. We do not gather thorns from grape-stalks. There are societies only nominally Christian Endeavor, and now and then Endeavor societies have "gone to seed" through lack of proper attention, but these are no more reflections on the movement than a worldly church or an unfaithful Christian is a reflection on Christianity.

The movement is a footprint of God in the progress of the ages. We stand upon the moors, windswept with sectarian controversy, and as we see the footprint, realize that God has passed that way. After him the flowers bloom, and the swirl of contention settles into the steadfast trades of interdenominational commerce. But all that has been accomplished is but a precursor of what is yet to be. The next step will be but in the same direction.

2. *There has been an advance in international fellowship.*—The fellowship of nations is doubtless not to be brought about by diplomacy or statecraft alone. It is one of the triumphs reserved for the gospel. By the gathering of Christian people from various lands, and by the spread of the Society among the nations of the earth, there is the propagation of a mutual love that will hasten the beating of the swords into ploughshares, and the spears into pruning-hooks. Christianity, with the Prince of peace at the head, must bring peace to the earth.

3. *A similar fellowship has been produced among the various parts of our own country through Christian Endeavor work.*—It would be an exaggeration to say that Christian Endeavor is to be named as the only force that promotes such fellowship; but its conventions attract persons from so wide a territory, and there is such a spirit of religious unity pervading the societies, that the influence is powerful on the side of a secular "union of heart and a union of hand." In the New York Convention, in the consecration meeting, the State of

Washington responded with the text, "As far as the east is from the west, so far hath he removed our transgressions from us." This object-lesson concerning God's forgiving love was very powerful, and swept over the heart like a new sense of his mercy. East and West were seen grasping hands in a convention in the interest of the spread of the gospel. There were two lessons from the incident: God's mercy for the sinner, and the power of the gospel to bring together the earth's "remotest bounds." So, too, is Christian Endeavor binding together the North and South; it is helping to make a flowery garland of Mason and Dixon's line, and there the honeysuckle and rose twine in sweet profusion.

CHAPTER III.

CONSTANT QUANTITIES AND NEW FACTORS.

It has well been said that, however much machinery may be improved, we cannot get away from certain mechanical principles and appliances.—There will be necessity for cogs and journals and bands, no matter how otherwise unique the machine may be. So in Christian Endeavor, there are certain quantities that must remain constant, no matter what improvement may be made in other directions.

1. *One of these constant quantities is system.*— No society or member is absolutely systematic in work. Much can be accomplished simply by improved system. Increased power is also needed. Nothing can be done without the power of the Holy Spirit. Nevertheless, many of the prayers for power are lazy prayers; they mean, when translated: "Lord, so arrange it that it will be easy for me to do my work. I do not like to exercise myself in conscious self-denial. It is hard to strive."

There can be no accession of power that will absolve us from the necessity of striving, or "keeping the body under." No martyr or prophet or apostle ever reached such a state; it is foreign to human conditions. We may attain great grace, but never can be rid of striving. What we should do is to systematize our efforts and harness our powers to the work. When on the bank of a rushing river, we should not pray for water, but rather for a water-wheel. Why pray for more ability, when there are pounds and talents wrapped up in napkins or buried in the earth? If we were to practise system, our usefulness would be multiplied, and then God would give more power.

The difference between a successful and unsuccessful person is often the difference between system and haphazard. Unemployed, "Jeshurun waxed fat and kicked," and there are many Christian people like Jeshurun: they need not more strength, but a harness! Efforts should be systematized until the margins of time are employed. A business man was asked to buy a fountain pen, on the plea that it would save his dipping his pen into the ink. He replied, "I do not want to use your pen; would you take away my only vacation?"

"But," one says, "you ask too much; you permit no respite at all, and would force us to a slavish routine."

By no means. System makes work easy; lack of system makes it hard. One who is sporadic in his efforts grows weary, and accumulated tasks discourage him. The suggestions now offered are for the comfort of the worker and the better performance of his duties. The body languishes and labor is hard when the system is out of order. This is the chief trouble with some societies;

their system is out of order.   It has been said,
"Work without haste, but work without rest."
If we work systematically, we can work continu-
ously.

I have been told, "You are always in a hurry."
"No," I have replied, "I am never in a hurry,
but I always keep going."   A river flows fastest
when it flows bank-full, and an individual will do
his best work when his time is all occupied and
his round of work up to the limit of his ability.

Some work all the time, but do not perform duties in their season.   Let us write a new proverb:
"Never do to-day what you can put off till to-
morrow!"   It is not advisable to do to-day all
that *can* be done to-day, but only that which
ought to be done to-day.

Here is a good rule for systematic workers: "Of
two duties that press upon you equally, do now
the one that can be done only now, and postpone
the one that can be postponed."   Many put off till
to-morrow what ought to be done to-day, and do
to-day what ought to be put off till to-morrow.

System requires discrimination.   Oliver Wendell
Holmes has said that "amusements are for children and fools."   He who properly adjusts his
tasks and changes his employment from one duty
to another in its season, will need so-called "recreation" no more than we need recreation from
being too healthy and happy.   But when the
system is out of order, all sorts of expedients
are necessary.

The pledge requires us to be systematic.—We
have promised to strive to do "whatever he

would like to have us do," and any one who believes that God would like him to be systematic, is thereby under a solemn pledge to strive for system in his life and work. Every one should turn to his toil with the firm determination to be systematic and to systematize his society's efforts, and thus employ all unused powers to the best advantage.

We do not do enough for God with such service as can be given in spare moments. Thought and plan must be put into the matter. They come far short of a perfect obedience who devote the best of their thought to the things of the world. With God and his work first, all other things will be added unto us. The constant quantity of system, when developed, becomes almost a new factor.

2. *Another constant quantity is the convention idea, and in its development this may be said to be a new force.*—Conventions are object-lessons to the world and sources of encouragement to Christians. The international gatherings are now so large that no one can see the whole convention. Neither does one see a modern battle between great armies. Only a portion of the field is in view from any one point; yet the army can be wielded as one. Those who attend these great convocations and are incommoded on account of the throngs, ought to rejoice that such outpourings are possible. They should be satisfied to be part of such a spectacle, even though they but help to swell the overplus; for the size of the overflow gives force and interest to the assemblage. On the other hand, it would be a matter for sorrow if all could

be comfortably accommodated. We serve the Lord when we merely increase the visibility of Christianity.

There is a power in simply "marching round Jericho"; such a season of marching may bring the shout and the crumbling of the walls. Not a few representatives only should march, but the multitude.

It may be said, "Other bodies have found it necessary to abandon the mass-convention idea, and so will Christian Endeavor." It may be replied, "Must we follow the trite representative method forever because in the past it has not been learned how to do otherwise?" The living throngs should beat back and forth through the land till the church of God shakes the gates of hell. Thus far we have only been playing at war. It is no time to call a halt because we have gone further than formerly. There should not be a reconnoissance in force and then retirement to the trenches. Something must come of the demonstrations commensurate with their size. Something *has* come of them; but we should not be content with small results from a great agency, nor be like that commander who

" With twenty thousand men
Marched up a hill, and then —— marched down again."

Aside from the purpose to live for Christ and the church, zeal is needed for immediate and thorough conquest. The host will be kept together and will increase, if at each step there is a new motive for further activity. A mere aggregation of parts will disintegrate; a movement acquires solidarity by the cohesive force of a felt need for further conquest. Action creates fellowship, and kneads the mass into an individual of whom each former individual is a part. The Endeavor movement should gather strength till all the church is in line with Christ and for Christ.

3. *The idea of pledged service is persistent; that is, conscious effort of the will must always be a factor in Christian life.*—Some duties should become habitual; indeed, each duty should become habitual in its turn; but he is not a progressive Christian all of whose duties are habitual. When his work becomes easy, he should seek harder work. When he can do all that the pledge seems to require, it is time to search for deeper meanings. There must always be duties that cost an effort, else where is the striving?

Of each sentence in the pledge two leading questions should be asked: "What does this mean to me?" "What ought it to mean?"

We may then particularize: "Have I sounded the depths of *trust?*" "Do I realize all that is meant by leading *a Christian life?*" "Have I comprehended what it is *to do as well as I know?*" In one way or another, the pledge idea must maintain its force at every stage of the Christian career, impelling to higher planes of experience and effort.

Critics may say that the pledge is a failure, that there are Endeavorers who do not keep the pledge, and whole societies that seem to have lost a proper conception of its demands. To this, answer may be made, that doubtless there are such Endeavorers and societies, and that this is precisely what must be expected unless another lesson is taken in the school of Christian effort.

It is not surprising that the pledge should fail; it always will fail, if it is made a basis for trust. This fact is just a revelation of a further need; it is a step in a process whereby we arrive at the ultimate source of strength. The earnest Endeavor worker who soberly and thoughtfully considers the great questions involved may rejoice that the tendency has been detected, in order that the remedy may be applied.

The following draft of the pledge, as some Endeavorers seem to understand it, may serve to illustrate, or characterize, not only a false conception of Endeavor obligations, but a too general failure on the part of many Christians to comprehend their profession of faith in Christ. The version is not altogether original, but is a growth, like the pledge itself.

THE PSEUDO-PLEDGE.

Trusting in myself for strength, I promise to do whatever I would like to do; that I will make it the rule of my life to pray and to read the Bible every day—except when I choose to omit it; and to support my own church in every way, especially by attending all her regular Sunday and midweek services, unless prevented by some inconvenience that I can twist into an excuse for not doing so; and that, just so far as I feel like it, throughout my whole life, I will endeavor to lead a Christian life.

As a passive member, I promise to be true to some of my duties; to be present at, and take some part, especially singing, in every Christian Endeavor prayer meeting, unless prevented by some reason that I can employ to silence my conscience. If I attend the monthly consecration meeting of the society, I will, if I do not forget it, read at least a verse of Scripture in response to my name at the roll-call, if some one is thoughtful enough to hand me a text for that purpose.

The explanation of this failure to comprehend the meaning of the pledge is, imperfect work by the lookout committee at the outset, in some instances; but in all cases the obligation of the pledge will have less and less weight with even the best-intentioned Endeavorers, unless they go a step further in their appreciation of its meaning than is at first possible.

The philosophy of the whole subject is: We are bulbous in our mental structure,—the mind is composed of the sensibilities, intellect, and will. Some persons live in the outer envelope, some in the second. Christian Endeavor reaches the will; but the will is still in the mind, and its energies will fail unless we go below the will to the " power behind the throne,"· the heart, which is in the spiritual nature. What is needed is a "heart tonic."

The pledge idea is a necessity, but not final; we must employ it, but must go beyond it. The writer has found his own will and word insufficient. Not till he learned to distrust his will and trust God was the victory won, and even now would he fall if relying on self.

No one need fear the duties that lie beneath the

surface of the pledge. Studied properly, the pledge
is found to contain the "heart tonic," or recipe
for its own proper observance. Trust in God,
prayer, Bible study, faithfulness to the services of
the church,—these are sufficient for the nourish-
ment of the daily life that is consecrated to God.

But how many fail to emphasize the thought of
trusting, and lay stress upon the "*I promise*"!
Herein is the fatal weakness. As soon as we
learn, however much of conscious surrender of
will there is in our case, that trust must not be in
the will, but in God, we shall reach the point
where the pledge idea can produce permanent
results. The will is used to undertake duties so
vast that the soul, trembling in conscious inability
to perform its work alone, flies to the divine
source for all its strength. The pledge idea,
therefore, must be a constant factor, but is only a
stepping-stone, not itself ultimate.

*At least two general thoughts appear prominent
in scanning the pledge for a conception of the higher
duties it implies.* One of them is the performance
of the "next duty," suggested in "whatever."
If Endeavorers were asked to promise to undertake the "next duty," they might hesitate, fearing that it would turn out to be the very one from
which they had been shrinking, or some other
equally hard. Yet, if we promise to strive to do
"whatever He would like to have us do," how can
we escape the next duty, which must surely be
part of the "whatever"? With such a view of
the case, self-adulation that we have kept the
pledge begins to vanish, and self-reproach, not un-

mingled with discouragement, begins to take its place. But as striving in God's strength in the past brought blessing, so will future striving. He who gives strength for the "whatever" will give strength for the "next duty" it includes.

The "whatever" also embraces soul-saving. Surely this is something God would like to have done. How can any one claim to have kept his pledge if he has not striven to bring immortal souls to eternal life? Surely God desires us to be ready for every good work, and to perform each duty as well as lieth in us, not merely as well as it suits our convenience. And none of these duties can be performed without an effort of the will, without a pledge, or resolution. Self-denial is a grace that must always inhabit the soul, but love, its twin, will nerve the will gladly to take up the burden.

4. *There are other factors, essentially constant and susceptible of a high degree of development.*— They are everywhere fundamental in the Christian system, such as interdenominational fellowship, loyalty to one's own church, the study of the Bible, and dependence on daily strength for daily needs.

CHAPTER IV.

THE SOCIETY OF THE INDIVIDUAL.

The times demand an advance in the apprehension of private responsibility. The study of this need and of the method of supplying it is almost a new department in applied theology.

There are certain considerations that may be urged to bring each person to the proper standard of activity.

1. *One of these is, the feasibility of our endeavors.—* It may be thought that the foregoing exposition of the demands of the pledge makes Christian service difficult; but it should be remembered that many of the "next duties" are small and easy, and that "what He would like to have us do" is often some plain thing liable to be overlooked in the desire to perform heroic actions. It is by performing simple duties that we get strength for larger ones.

A young man thought he ought to be a minister, but those who knew him best believed that he was not qualified for such work. By and by he found a line of usefulness; he made an excellent errand-boy for some other Christian worker. He was a good man to carry a note, or to remind residents that there would be a cottage prayer meeting in the next block, and ask them to come.

Many persons could be useful in humble ways, but never realize that they are to do simple things. God needs a multitude of errand-boys and errand-girls. A pastor is unable to compass all his work. He needs as many eyes as Argus, as many hands as Briareus, and as many feet as a centipede. The next time the Endeavorer sings,—

> "Take my feet and let them be
> Swift and beautiful for thee,"

let him take his feet to the pastor's house, and say, "Pastor, have you any work for two such feet as these?" and he will tell of journeys to take, of neighborhoods to traverse, of errands to run. The two feet may be just as useful as the pastor's head, if they carry out what the head plans. When one sings,—

> "Take my hands and let them move
> At the impulse of thy love,"

let him take his hands to the pastor and say, "Pastor, is there anything you want these two hands to do?" He will tell of invitations to write, of lists to copy, of leaflets to distribute. The two hands may be as useful as the pastor's head, if they execute what the head plans. The pastor is a multiplicand; the members should be the multiplier. Would God like you to act in this capacity? Then, there is your duty, and likewise your opportunity. The pounds and talents that are hidden away are often such as have been named, and would increase if used.

2. *A second consideration is that of simple obliga-*

tion or duty.—It has been said that we should not wish for a modern David to slay the modern Goliath, but should rather desire the armies of God, in their rank and file, to be brave enough not to shrink from Philistine brag and bluster. How much better would it be if the whole church were composed of Davids who would fight as one man! The result sought should be the uplifting of the people of God to the right plane of action. It would be much more to the credit of Christianity if the church should arise spontaneously against all evil, rather than that a champion should appear to save the trembling hosts.

There can not be an accomplishment of all that should be done till the individual feels his responsibility. Only when each member realizes that everything that can be said of the Endeavor movement applies to himself will the real spring of action be reached. The discussion must be narrowed to the individual till he is transformed from a spectator into a moving force, impelled by a consciousness both of his importance and his supreme obligation. Each should ask, not merely, "What is the next step for Endeavor?" but, "What is *my* next step? What would the Lord have *me* do?" When Christians arrive at this point, not many will stand idle, unable to distinguish their duty.

Some one has suggested the abolition of all societies, and the formation instead of the "Society of the Individual." Such a method would lead to ecclesiastical anarchy, but this "society" is needed *in addition* to all others. Man is a microcosm; that is, a little universe. He is directly responsible to God, and carries daily and hourly obligations. He should form out of this microcosm the "Society of the Individual," elect himself its president, secretary, treasurer, and committees, and set himself to work.

Many are afraid of duty because they do not fully believe God. There is a parable, generally misinterpreted, concerning the laborers in the vineyard, some of whom went to work at the first hour, and some as late as the eleventh. This parable was not intended to teach that men should not remain idle until the eleventh hour, for those who began to work at that time did so on the first opportunity that was presented; but the parable was constructed to bring out a certain other truth. If the context is studied, it will be plain that the parable meant to condemn a bargaining spirit. Those who wrought but one hour received as much as those who worked twelve. The latter had bargained for a penny a day; the former did not bargain at all, but trusted the promise of the master to pay what was right. This made it right for him to reward them with as large a wage as was given those who had toiled the whole day in a less commendable spirit.

3. *We must not be bargaining Christians, demanding of God a fixed wage before entering his service.*—He who bargains for a penny will get it, *but only a penny.* He who waits till assured that the work will be of such and such character, and that he will get this or that reward,—till satisfied on a bargaining basis,—can never know the

full joy of the Christian life. But they who believe that God can be trusted to assign appropriate duties, give grace to perform them and reward sufficient for the toil, will embrace the first opportunity for service, labor joyfully to the end, and receive the largest recompense.

Faith in God means faith in his work; joy in him means joy in his work. A lagging step betrays the presence of doubt. When the point of true individual consecration of the "Society of the Individual" is reached, the church will be prepared for all things, for God can then use his people to the full limit of their responsibility and opportunity.

PART II.—Special Features.

After this general survey, we should look more particularly into certain features of the work, studying closely and analytically, with a view to higher spiritual conceptions. This treatment is intended to be suggestive, to further the application of the general idea to remaining lines of thought.

CHAPTER I.

PLEDGE MEANINGS.

Each phrase of the pledge will bear careful examination. Its ideas are capable of indefinite expansion. Instead of gliding over the surface, let us pause for deep sea sounding, to bring up treasures from the depths.

1. *Trusting.*—The Christian should know better each day what this means, and realize more and more its importance and blessedness. The necessity for trust and the sweetness of trust should both be grasped; we should trust God because we love him, because he is worthy to be trusted, because we dare not trust ourselves. To trust is not to dismiss personal responsibility; it does not mean carelessness or absence of thought; it is an active principle, the sentiment of hearts

striving for a better life. We trust for strength, not ease. *True trusting leads to striving.*

2. *I promise.* — One's word should be sacred. Another meaning of promise is "pledge," the meaning in the case before us. Woe to him who breaks his word! It is like the destruction of the reflector behind a light. The Endeavor promise is not given to the society, but to God. We promise *him*. Nor does it expire by a statute of limitation. Most of the pledge is for duties that cannot be laid aside, even though one cease to be a member of the society. *The promise* should be made "*trusting.*"

3. *Strive.* — This word gives name to the Endeavor Society. To strive, the effort must be honest and continuous. Endeavor means the opposite of inaction and selfishness. *To strive to do,* one should "*trust for strength.*"

4. *Whatever.* — This means not a picking and choosing of agreeable duties, but the performance of hard and easy, exalted and lowly, pleasing and distasteful, obligations. No one is fully consecrated till he is at the point of doing the *whatever. He who trusts will find his promise impel him to strive in all directions.*

5. *He would like to have me do.* — We are to seek to please God, not to do what we *must* do, but what he would *wish* us to do. The truly obedient child is not forced to duty, but seeks to carry out the desires of father and mother. The Endeavorer with a tender conscience cannot do what the Lord would not like to have him do, or omit to do what He would like done. Our promise is

not only to obey the commands of Christ, *but to follow his desires, and we are to trust and strive to this end.*

6. *To pray and read the Bible every day.*—Every Christian knows that God does not like him to do these things in a perfunctory or formal way; and, according to promise, we are to strive to do them as He would like,—eagerly, conscientiously, profitably. Higher ideas of prayer and of the study of God's word are essential to progress in the Christian life. They are the food to supply soul need. *No one can truly trust God for strength, if he neglect prayer and the study of the Word.*

7. *To support my own church in every way.*—This is also promotive of trust. Church attendance is regarded by some as a comparatively small matter. They may acknowledge that by failure to support the church in every way they do really break the pledge, but still assert that living a Christian life is the important thing, as though a broken pledge were consistent with a Christian life!

A Christian life is not an abstraction. It includes all the particulars of service. If one believes that God would like him to support his own church in every way, then he is pledged to *strive* thus to support his church. The society exists "for Christ and the church," and "by their fruits ye shall know them." God established the church, and no one can afford to neglect that which God has seen necessary to establish. *Faithfulness to the church is a means of fostering trust.* No one should say "I trust," and then neglect God's ordinance.

8. *Conscientiously.*—How many sins that word has cloaked! Inclination is often taken for conscience, and the reason, or excuse, is given to that instead of to God. It ought not to be said, "If you can satisfy your conscience, do thus and so." No one has a conscientious reason till he can go to God with it and satisfy him. The case is not between a man and his conscience, but between his conscience and God. If God would like us to do a thing, it is proof that there is no real hindrance to its performance. *Instead of using conscience to prevent striving, we are to use conscience to increase striving.* A conscience that does not impel to effort and self-denial is a bad conscience. Those who are true to all the preceding phrases of the pledge will likely be truly conscientious; the others, not.

9. *True to all my duties.*—This means more than the duties that pertain to the society meetings; it includes all committee duties and all matters connected with the business affairs of the society, and, indeed, all the work that an Endeavorer should do, as outlined in the whole pledge. Emphasis should be laid on "*true,*" as well as on "*all.*" To be *true* precludes the idea of slighting the work, and implies the exhibition, not only of faithfulness, but of enthusiasm and of painstaking exactness. It means the honest fulfilment of every worthy purpose, trusting in the Lord for strength. *To do all precludes the idea of selecting those duties which are most agreeable.*

CHAPTER II.

WHAT IT IS TO LEAD A CHRISTIAN LIFE.

Ideas of the Christian life should not remain stationary. Our Christian endeavor is not confined to a set period; it is not only persistent, but cumulative. Our lives should be lives of striving. A Christian life means a Christian *life*, not a fragment of one; it means regular and growing powers, not fits and starts of animation; it means constant assimilation of good materials and the bearing of fruit, not rudimentary existence or sterile blossoms on the boughs.

When an Endeavorer promises, so far as he knows how, to lead a Christian life, he has entered upon a service that is up to the limit of his possibilities and opportunities.—When first taken, this promise often suggests to the mind no more than a generality; but he who truly *endeavors* will speedily come to a better comprehension of every phase of his pledge, and will realize that to lead a Christian life means a multitude of things, and a tense, but not joyless, employment of every power. There must be training into a comprehension of what it means to live for God. Ideals must not be low, nor should there be contentment with the ordinary and conventional operations.

A Christian life, lived as far as we know, means:—

1. *Not to live it less perfectly than we know.*—
Many do come short of their known duties. They
are persuaded that certain lines of conduct are not
conducive to their highest good, yet follow them
on the plea that it makes but slight difference,
till, by doing them, they have broken their pledge
to live up to their highest conceptions. Duties
and responsibilities that plainly should be discharged are often neglected. He who does not do
as well as he knows, does not live the Christian
life to the full. Sins of omission are often more
grievous than sins of commission. If every professed Christian lived up to his actual light, there
would be an uplift in church work such as the
world has not seen since Pentecost. He who
knew his duty, and did it not, was to be beaten
with many stripes, and we shall be judged if we
come short of doing "as well as we know." But
to lead a Christian life means:—

2. *To strive to know better.*—There must be
advance in thought as well as deed. An earnest performance of known duty will create a
hunger and thirst that can be satisfied only by
clearer vision of God's will. When we remember
that the thorough performance of known duty includes prayer, the study of God's Word, personal
work for the salvation of souls, faithfulness to the
public services, self-denial, and heart-searching,
we comprehend how there must naturally result a
desire to know our duty and experience God's
grace more perfectly. It is evident also, upon
slight reflection, that one known duty is to seek to
grow in grace. When the fire of consecration is

kindled in the heart, it will produce a zeal for progress in all things that exalt God's glory and make us more efficient in his service.

The model for the Christian's progress is found in the Beatitudes.—From the first step of humility up to enduring persecution for righteousness' sake, there are advancing phases of experience. The Christian begins with a contrite spirit, which he carries with him all the way, and ends a hero for God. If self-denying service has brought joy thus far in our Christian life, why should we hesitate about repeating the process for the years to come? It is always better further on. If we have made some attainment, we should, like Paul, forget the "things that are behind," in the sense of not being satisfied with them, and press toward the high goal.

3. *The Christian life is one of added blessing*, and all its service is reasonable. It is homogeneous, not joy to a certain point, and grief afterwards. When an Endeavorer promises to lead a Christian life as long as he lives, he is entering into a state that is heaven below, if true to his vows, but a state that is full of complaint and half-hearted enjoyment, if false to them.

All the other promises of the pledge are but differentiations of this one, or subordinate features of it. To raise societies to the proper level, there should be held before them this full idea of the Christian life, not some fragment of it; its meaning, joy, and triumph, with Christ as the perfect example.

A Christian should be like a cube, and wherever

placed should exhibit the same symmetrical pro-
portions.   This symmetry he can attain only by a
growing appreciation of the fact that he is "saved
to serve," and that his service is to be applied, not
to the salvation of a few individuals, but to that of
the whole world,

CHAPTER III.

I. The Meaning of Consecration.—Next to entire dependence on divine power, consecration of the life is the great essential to success. "*A heart consecrated to God and dependent on God,*" *is the formula for the highest attainment in service.* Yet how many come short of the proper conception of the second, as well as the first, of these ingredients! Few words are more frequently used and more poorly understood than "consecration." And it is no wonder, when we reflect that there is very little comprehensive instruction on the subject. Members are told that they ought to be consecrated; and delinquents are reminded that they "have been missed" from the consecration meeting, but comparatively little is said about the meaning or joy of real consecration.

Consecration is not the making of promises; the promise is a product. Nor is it a formal ceremony performed once a month, though the meeting is held monthly. It is the spirit of service, not the formal annunciation of a purpose.

I shall endeavor to hold up a high idea of consecration.—I dare not do otherwise. It would be wrong to write on such a subject and then present but a misleading travesty. Madame Roland, on her way to execution, passed the statue of Liberty, and exclaimed, "O Liberty! Liberty! how many crimes are committed in thy name!" So we might exclaim, "O consecration! how many crimes are committed in thy name!"

Persons rise and say, "I consecrate myself," when they only mean, "I wish I could consecrate myself." Consecration is not a mere flutter of an emotion, a passing gush of feeling. It is the travail of a soul in the birth of a higher experience, the exquisite sense of crucifixion coupled with resurrection.

Moses said to the children of Israel, "Consecrate yourselves to-day to the Lord." It was a consecration of son against father, of brother against brother—to gird on the sword and slay, that a people might be purged of idolatry. Our consecration differs in direction, but should be of equal intensity—a consecration to save life, not to take it, a consecration of the son *for* the father, of brother *for* brother. If we would thrive as Christians, we must lay upon our souls the longing for the highest and best experiences. We should continue to discuss the best methods of work, but should seek more earnestly to produce that state of heart which is essential to the success of any method.

We might define consecration as the "spirit of eager performance of hard service for God, in dependence on his power."

There are several characteristics that mark real consecration.

1. *First of all, it is finding God's way.*—No life can be said to be consecrated all of whose activi-

ties are not consciously placed under his direction. To let God choose for us in every particular is an attribute. The *life*, not a portion of it, must be placed on the altar. We begin with consecration, not with consecrations. The mistake is often made of taking up this or that duty and imagining that because it requires some consecration the life belongs to God, when the whole life has never been given to him unreservedly. Not to choose for ourselves, but to trust his choice, to be willing to go anywhere, to do anything, and do it as he shall command,—this is consecration. We must not find some of God's ways, but *God's way*, and yield our hearts, even if we have not the slightest idea as to what he may direct us to do; his specific directions will be given after we have come to the point of willingness to do his will.

2. *Consecration must be perpetual.* — To forget our vows does not abrogate them. Duty is always duty until performed. Obligation is as persistent as opportunity. Doubtless, many soldiers who enlisted in the hundred-day service were brave men, for some of them died on the field of battle, and others were willing to sacrifice their lives; but when a man served his hundred days and re-enlisted, knowing what war was, there was no doubt as to the persistence of his purpose.

At the battle of Gettysburg, the Confederate general, J. B. Gordon, learning that a Federal general had been shot, rode to the place indicated, and found the wounded officer to be General Barlow, who had been shot through from front to back, and was able to speak only in a whisper.

General Gordon, acting upon what seemed a dying request, sent certain articles from the person of his fallen foe to Mrs. Barlow, who was at the time at Meade's headquarters, distant a dozen miles or more, and in kindness conveyed the General within the Confederate lines, where he might receive such medical relief as was possible for one suffering from a mortal wound. In the night Mrs. Barlow appeared, asking for permission to visit her husband. This was readily granted, and the faithful wife and brave warrior soon passed from the knowledge of the equally brave Southern general and timely friend. After the war had been concluded, General Gordon, in attendance at a banquet in a Northern State, found himself at the table with a certain General Barlow. As two General Gordons and two General Barlows had fought in the war, General Barlow remarked to the Southern soldier, "I suppose you are not the General Gordon who was killed in North Carolina?" "No, sir," was the reply, "I am not, but I fought all through the war; it was my nephew who was killed in North Carolina. I suppose, sir, you are not the General Barlow I killed at Gettysburg?" "Yes," was the reply, "I am the General Barlow you killed at Gettysburg!" The sequel showed that he had recovered of his wound, gone back to the front, and added new laurels to his brow. It is hardly necessary to say that the two generals rose from the table, and, clasped in each other's arms, gave expression to that emotion which could be the product only of such exceptional circumstances.

That was perpetual consecration; and it matters not how many times the Christian has been shot through on the battle-field of life, he should again go back to the front. There is no discharge in this war; there are no excuses for inaction; our devotion must be undying; as long as there is an enemy in arms, our place is in the line of battle. The scars of conflict will but emphasize our devotion and make our example more powerful. Particular duty may change, the direction of efforts be altered, but the consecration must be a permanent fact in the life.

3. *Consecration should be progressive.* — The twelfth chapter of Romans emphasizes the idea. First, it describes the yielding of the life to God; next, the specific lines of service; and then presents a long list of particular duties. The conception of obligation should become more distinct as we advance. Pentecost did not fit the early church for all its duties. Later on, the church learned what at first it could not comprehend, that the gospel was for the Gentiles also. Peter, though he preached at Pentecost so that three thousand souls were converted, afterward temporized, and was rebuked by Paul. No matter how blessed are our experiences, " still there's more to follow."

The writer remembers thinking, when a child, that boys were men when they were six years old. Such was the childish comprehension of life. In our educational career, the summit of useful knowledge seems, at first, to be just beyond the district school, then at the close of the college course. It is well that we cannot see from the beginning all that is to be learned, for the contemplation would forever discourage.

In climbing a mountain chain, one sees a higher range beyond. So God reveals difficulties by degrees, as Christians are able to bear them. He does not show the new-born Christian at once all the self-denials he must make, nor all the hard duties he must perform, for the sight would paralyze effort. As we gain one summit and see another just ahead, there is nothing to do but get down into the valley of humiliation, where we find sweet refreshment to help us climb again on the other side. The Christian steps from the level of earth's highest range into the portals of heaven.

True consecration means constant endeavor. When a Christian ceases to strive, he ceases to be consecrated. Growth in grace is only another term for progressive consecration.

4. *Consecration is thoughtfulness.*—It does not begin when some one has done our thinking for us and convinced us of our duty, but it includes the employment of the thinking powers in all seriousness, to find duty. Beau Brummel was asked how he managed to tie his necktie so neatly. He replied that he "put his mind to it." So it is impossible for us to do anything well unless we "put our minds to it." No consecration is complete that does not include the mind.

A false view of the duty of young people in this respect has been industriously propagated. Frequently we hear such statements as, "You cannot put old heads on young shoulders," "You must not expect too much of young people." I have seen a list of entertainments prepared for "young people," and, in over thirty, only one was religious in character, and a number were designed to be comic. A song-book, prepared to fill a long-felt want, to furnish something in "consonance with young life," and issued in the name of religious work, contains a number of effusions most ridiculous in character.

This treatment of the capacity of the young is hurtful to their spiritual growth. We underestimate them, and treat them as though they were essentially foolish. Yet these same young people master abstruse problems in the schools, and show ability to grapple with hard subjects in mathematics and language. Do they study Greek because it is excruciatingly funny? Does the young pupil study arithmetic because the multiplication table is a huge joke? Why should it be said of the young, who thus show their powers of thought to be superior to those of many who are older, that they cannot be expected to be thoroughly devoted in their religious life or comprehend the "deep things of God"? Away with this pernicious doctrine, which has been disproved over and over again in every age of the world's history! Contrast with it Paul's word to Timothy: "Let no man despise thy youth; but be thou an example of the believers, in word, in conversation, in charity, in spirit, in faith, in purity. . . . Meditate upon these things; give thyself wholly to them; that thy profiting may appear to all." It would be most helpful to all young people, if

they would master the contents of the epistles to
Timothy. O the joy of a life that early learns
the mysteries of divine grace, and couples the
glow of youth with the deep peace of the abiding
presence of the Holy Spirit!

5. *Consecration, at its limit, is crucifixion.*—He
who continually follows Christ will find his Cal-
vary. Consecration means soul travail. It is not
a life of compromise, but of martyrdom. The
path of life is a narrow path, just as wide as the
bleeding feet of Christ. Perhaps it is Bishop Foss
who says, in substance: "Sometimes there is such
affliction in the life that it seems as though the
heartstrings would break. Never mind; it is
only God tuning you up to a higher key."

The harp of our heart is very much unstrung,
and we almost rebel against the touches of God's
tender fingers that would straighten out the sensi-
tive tangle. The tuning is like the tuning of a
piano long neglected. The tuner says, "I cannot bring it up to pitch at once, but will do the
best I can to-day, and go over it again a few days
later." So God goes over our hearts again and
again, and each new consecration brings us more
and more into harmony with all the harps of
heaven. The exquisite pain is the momentary
dissonance that resolves in the next note into the
most thrilling concord. Why should we shrink
from the process that initiates us into bliss? We
should not turn back from the supreme moment.

This leads to the thought:—

6. *Consecration is not submission, but commission.*—The word "submit" does not occur in the

Bible as describing the proper attitude of the believing soul toward God, in the sense of yielding
to compulsion. We must not bow reluctantly to
his will because we think we cannot help ourselves, but should *commit* our souls to him as to a
faithful Creator. A Christian should not be lifted
to the altar as to a surgeon's table, but should
quickly ascend as to a banquet. God loves the
cheerful giver, whether he gives money or service.
Consecration should be with gladness and confidence, else it loses much of its character as consecration. Is the gift of life without love a real
gift? It is the mockery of selfishness.

7. *Consecration is the door of real enjoyment.*—It
affords the opportunity to acquire true joy and
blessing. The poet sings of the

> "Pure delight of a *single hour*
> That before thy cross I spend."

What must be the delight of a *life* of the same
character? To live in the world, yet wholly apart
from it, is not gloomy, for such lives are lived with
God.

Men look at the worthies of the past, and exclaim at the peculiar blessedness of their careers;
but those lives were made different by consecration, and others may enter into the same life by
the same process.

The Matterhorn is one of the most difficult peaks
in Europe to ascend. One who had reached the
summit was asked concerning the view. His reply
was, "Mountain-climbers do not ascend for the
view, but for the climb." There is something in

the familiarity with mountain desolation, in the poise of mind gained, and in the mastery of self in perilous situations, that pays for the trouble. So the Christian is blessed in himself by the effort put forth, and, besides, feasts his soul on the view which always appears from the summit of consecration.

Chalmers, in one of his famous "astronomical sermons," said that if one of the islands of the blest were to float by, how eagerly watchers would desire to pass over the narrow gulf and join the happy throngs! To-day it is no "island of the blest" that draws near, but the life of consecration. The drawbridge is let down; we may step over if we will. What shall we choose, that life or this?

Consecration presents transcendent possibilities for each of us. All things may be ours, if we are willing to have them. Let each think of himself as he is, and then as he ought to be. It is the service of God alone that presents a field for the highest attainment.

It has been said that an infant can climb to any height, if only the steps are made short enough. In the consecrated life, the duties God sends are steps suited to the feet.

Isaiah saw the Lord, whose train filled the temple. When the seraph cried, the door-posts moved, and Isaiah exclaimed that he was undone, for he was of unclean lips, and dwelt with a people of unclean lips, and had seen the Lord of hosts. Then a seraph touched his lips with a coal from the altar, and told him that his iniquity was taken away;

and when the Lord said, "Whom shall I send?"
the same Isaiah replied, "Here am I; send me."
To be consecrated, we must feel God's power and
our own unworthiness, and then he will consecrate
us, and we shall be ready to go; but we cannot
consecrate ourselves.

The death of the consecrated Christian will be
as glorious as the ascent of Elijah. Though no
whirlwind envelop him, the life on the altar will be
as a perfume, mounting higher and higher. When
the last ember has been consumed, the final wreath
of incense will disengage itself as silently as a
breath of evening, and float upward till lost in the
opening of heaven; and the Elisha left behind will
take up the mantle and go forth to even greater
deeds for God.

II. The Consecration Meeting.

1. *As a means of promoting consecration, the
consecration meeting is most important.* — The
statement has been made that the consecration
meeting is wrong in principle and inefficient in
operation. This conclusion is doubtless due to a
misapprehension of the purpose of the meeting,
and to occasional bad methods in its conduct; but
it shows the liability of the consecration meeting
to dangers from without and within the society,
and calls for a speedy exaltation of the true idea
in the minds of all Endeavorers.

It has been objected that we can make but one
consecration of our lives; that in this respect consecration is like being born, and that there is no
such thing as being born again and again.

But it is evident that some things must be done over and over. Consecration is never beyond our present light. If we are to consecrate ourselves but once, why not make just one prayer in our life, that God will direct us in every conceivable circumstance, and then never pray again? Why not read the Bible through carefully just once, and read it no more? While the consecration at the beginning of our Christian life should be complete as to a full surrender of heart for service, definite duties arise from time to time that were not in the mind at the first. These must be taken up—and that is consecration—just as new prayers are made for new supplies of strength for daily needs.

Every one knows that his earlier views of the Christian life were crude, and that with the advent of new light, and the vision of new duties, there had to come a conscious yielding, often a conscious struggle, to do the will of God. The Christian's life is marked all the way with mementos of battle-fields through which he has passed.

There should be a care about saying, "*I reconsecrate myself*"; for, although one may and should return to the right way after having wandered, yet consecration should not be primarily for duties once assumed but not performed, nor is the consecration meeting for the purpose of securing strength to perform neglected vows, but for an advance in service and life. It is by the steady progress in the performance of *new* duties that we are enabled to bring up the rear of our scattered forces.

Say to the Endeavorers that there should be no

consecration meeting, and many will take it as a
call to abandon serious thought and heartfelt
devotion. One of the worst ills that could happen
to the movement would be the abandonment of
methods because in some cases they had been
poorly managed.

*The necessity for periods of searching the heart is
apparent.* Special occasions are helpful to produce
results that are supposed to be continuous. If
there should be services of any kind, why not services to hold up to view the higher plane of living,
to lead to introspection, to bring the personal life
into the full blaze of God's perfect will concerning it?

Leave out the idea of self-examination, and
cease to educate the people on that subject by
public services especially suited to the purpose,
and there will be an eradication of an element
that is fundamental to spiritual growth. We
must guard and elevate the consecration meeting.
Satan will try to diminish its power, that it may
be abandoned altogether; and then what?

2. *There are cases where the consecration meeting
has become formal;* but is it strange that this
should occur, when less thought has been put into
this particular service than into almost any other,
so far as a careful study of its character and possibilities is concerned? There must be education
as to its true meaning. It is the heart of the
society, as the pledge is the backbone. The complaint from which many societies suffer is heart
disease.

The ideas that lie along the line of this subject

relate to the whole matter of Christian progress. Consecration means frankness with one's self. It means the taking up of harder duties. It means Christian helpfulness drawn from the deep well of personal experience rather than from admonition.

The service may be called by some other name if the fact be retained; but better than to change the name is to put the right content into it. Leaders should study not so much the topic as to develop the spirit of consecration. The word "consecration" need not be used every time the individual desires to express a purpose in line with the idea; the essential thing is that the heart should feel a genuine uplift for future life and service. [See "Consecration" under "Methods" and "Union Work."]

PART III.—METHODS.

CHAPTER I.

GENERAL OBSERVATIONS.

New ideas in methods are constantly being evolved: or perhaps it would be better to say that new ways of working are constantly being *discovered*, and that the true principles that underlie all methods are better comprehended each year. To do everything in the name of Christ and by the power of the Holy Spirit is the one true method.

There are a few general observations that may prove suggestive as to present needs and efforts:

1. Endeavor methods should embrace those things that contribute to the immediate welfare, not only of the society, but also, more and more, of the church activities. The Endeavorer's horizon will constantly widen as he ascends to higher planes of personal living.

2. The methods should include systematic, not piecemeal, Bible study.

3. Training for personal work in the saving of souls, with the aim to make the Endeavorers more earnest, persistent, systematic, and skilful, should be an object.

4. The application of all this to the life of the

citizen, in the Christian-citizenship movement, and to the salvation of the world, through missionary effort, is a logical and necessary result.

In the discussion of methods which follows, the writer gives in each case what he considers *as a rule, and in ordinary circumstances,* the best method; but wishes to be understood as urging the necessity for studying conditions and varying the method to suit contingencies that may arise. Sometimes it is not only advisable but necessary to substitute one method for another, and perhaps, later on, to return to the method first employed. In a former text-book, "How," this matter has received attention, but needs a reference here, that the intent of this chapter may not be misunderstood.

CHAPTER II.

Guide-boards, or principles of action, to which we refer in our ordinary work, as well as in emergencies, are needed to keep the worker in the path of progress. One of them concerns

I. The Worker's Equipment.

This includes the improvement of every faculty, every power. It requires about the same qualities to make a great orator as a great musician or poet. There must be a sense of sublimity, a power of expression, constructive ability, and tact. The Christian worker needs a wide grasp of truth, a conception of the greatness of his mission, and all the ability that the orator possesses or the musician employs; that is, all these powers can be used, and no worker ought to feel that he has prepared himself in the highest degree until he has educated his whole nature.

A harp, to make the sweetest music, must be thoroughly tuned. A young man who was getting an education said he thought he could wheel a barrow of bricks a little straighter because he knew something of geometry! Every item of useful knowledge can be employed in God's work. To be successful workmen for God, we must know something besides methods,—we must know principles. Endeavor culture should be as wide as Christian knowledge. A fully equipped Endeavorer is simply a fully equipped Christian.

1. *We must know God, by his Word and by experience; we must know ourselves; and we must know others.*—The worker must have a grasp of far-reaching and basic truths. To *master any portion of* a subject, one must at least *understand the whole subject.*

Christian work deals with every variety of experience and with all kinds of dispositions. It has to do with the most desperate cases of human depravity, and aims to lead the souls of men to the greatest of all heights. It teaches the most profound wisdom, and enters into the consideration of the divine mysteries. Can one for a moment think that this requires only cursory attention and shallow preparation? Still, any one who has the requisite faith may be used mightily of God, for the Holy Spirit will give wisdom if the worker truly seeks it.

2. *In addition to all this, the worker needs a perfect command of himself.*—A soldier is not thoroughly reliable until he is steady under fire. A mere knowledge of the drill will not suffice; he must have courage and coolness. These are the attributes that win victories. So the Christian worker must have steadiness, coolness, and courage. Otherwise, his followers may become panic-stricken. These qualities are not to be secured by attendance upon a training-school. One must have himself well in hand, or, rather, he must let God

have him in hand, that he may not spoil by precipitancy what he has gained by knowledge.

The worker must have character behind all his knowledge. No one is fully equipped until he is seasoned. Good material is not fit for a place in a building until it has been cured. In schools of methods, some plan should be employed for seasoning the workers.

3. *Continuity of purpose is a grace that is often lacking.*—Most persons become impatient if they cannot see the end from the beginning; yet one should not wish to apprehend all the difficulties that must be encountered, the trials, and intermediate disappointments. We can meet each trial singly, if we do not know that others are to follow; but what should we do if we saw the whole line of difficulties at once? On the other hand, we should become indolent if our preview disclosed no special obstacles.

We must take our work as we do the atmosphere,—one breath at a time. But by not pursuing an idea to its logical and necessary conclusion, we may make all our preceding endeavors ridiculous. The proof of the correctness of a course of conduct often lies in the result alone, and not until its last item has been reached can we convince objectors that we were right. Giving up too soon is often taken as a confession of error. We should not only have right principles, but we should possess perseverance. Consistency is a jewel that is set in the golden ring of constancy.

A line of policy that is not immediately successful may nevertheless be the most commendable one. Not everything can be made to yield its fruition at once. Blessed is he who continues in the work that will eventually bring forth the best results, rather than turn to some mushroom method to win present applause; and blessed is he who has patience to wait on such a worker, and encouragement for him. The worker needs some far-reaching plans. He who does only the present duty, without laying upon his soul the burden of a victory ultimately to be gained, is like the man who lives from hand to mouth and thinks he is provident.

Every difficulty in our path is a compendium of secrets. Its solution solves many other problems. It is like any other lesson, and enriches our knowledge when once mastered.

We cannot cultivate patience unless there are some things to try our patience; hence discouraging seasons are means of spiritual upbuilding. When growth in the church is not apparent, it may be just the time of ripening for the grain. We cannot develop courage unless there are duties that demand courage. Nor can knowledge be acquired without experiences to reveal ignorance. To cease demanding visible success at every turn, and to look upon trials as blessings, are preliminary steps in the way of continual progress. Too many persons long for the impossible, and so secure the unsubstantial.

4. *Thoroughness is necessary.*—Successful workers dig deep into the mines of truth. The surface of the earth will raise good crops for a while, but the process " of skinning the land " brings poverty

afterward. A depth of soil must be secured by deep ploughing, or underdraining, to ensure continued harvests. So some churches and societies grow lean by "skinning the land"; they use methods that are good for present results, but have no basis for future success. Lazily they do the easy thing, and reap the rewards of sluggishness.

This thoroughness must apply first to the Christian's own life.

As he painfully sends down his roots into the truth, somehow he joyfully sends up branches into the sky. Much of a Christian's life is secret and painstaking; but the more of it is hidden, the more of it is visible.

5. *The worker should have regard to the work of others.*—King David prepared for the building of the temple, but Solomon was to "add thereto." So it is our duty to prepare for those who follow us in any line of work, that they may bring it to the success we could not attain, rather than to hope that, for our own selfish honor, no one will be found quite as efficient as ourselves. It is our duty, also, to add to the heritage received, rather than to say, "Here is success enough already achieved, and there is nothing I need do except to take mine ease." In some sense, we are to be both David and Solomon combined, preparing lines of work for those who are to follow, and completing other lines already begun.

6. *There must be the equipment of power.*—This is not mere effectiveness in speech. The disciples were to be given power to be *witnesses*; that is,

insight into the truth, courage to maintain it, and fortitude and trust in their service. Because of an improper understanding of what power is, many have looked for results from their work that never were promised, and have given up in despair.

Power is finding a field. The disciples, when they received power, knew what they were to do, and where they were to do it. Finding a work is one manifestation of power.

Power is satisfaction with the work God gives us. The disciples were content to miss knowing the times and seasons, and to do the work given them, when they got power. So the Christian who has genuine power takes up his tasks cheerfully, and frets no more because of disappointments.

Power is varied in spiritual things as in nature. It is sometimes seen in the cyclone, and just as truly in the silent processes of growth. To maintain a cause in one field may require as much power as to carry on a cause elsewhere to a visible triumph. To plan a work, to be steady in times that try men's souls, to stand at one's post, to endure affliction, to bear unjust criticism,—these are all exhibitions of power. Power has no froth at the top, and no sediment at the bottom.

The life should have power, not merely the words and actions. There is power in character, in poise, in the outlines of one's career. Christians should be persons of power, in the true apostolic sense, in faithfulness, in trust, in patience, in self-mastery, in endowment from on high.

To be thus powerful, there must be self-surrender, not mere prayer. There will still be need of all that comes from prayer, the study of the Bible, humility, chastening, and growth in grace. No gift of power absolves from these. Power to be witnesses means equipment for service, and such service has a power far in excess of appearances.

II. Nature's Methods.

To study God's methods is essential.

1. *One reason why we do not attempt more for God, is because we do not* stand in awe of him as we ought. We should seek to appreciate his power, and then we shall venture at his command. We learn to know an artist by seeing his works, not principally by reading a review of his life. So we come to know God, not alone by studying the Bible, but by studying his works in nature and in grace. Communion with the works of God will assist materially in forming those conceptions that are necessary to the most effective service. The lightning is a type of his swiftness; the crags and peaks are silent witnesses of his might. As we behold his glory, we feel the inspiration of service.

2. *The physical universe is full of lessons* for him who works for souls. A thunder-shower that dashes through the sky is necessarily of short duration, while a steady rain generally begins gradually. The two types of rainfall illustrate two types of workers. We depend most upon the steady, patient forces, but still need the thunderstorm with its accompaniment of lightning.

God has use for all kinds of methods. An artificial standard must not be erected. God does not send all the rain at one time, nor all the fruit in one month. He teaches the lesson of adjusting efforts to recurring needs rather than finishing every piece of work at once, and "being done with it."

Our work, like nature's processes, is interwoven in such fashion that to do one thing we must do several others measurably. We are weavers; we handle certain threads, and then take up others that had been temporarily laid down. In this way the pattern grows. The painter mixes his colors and takes up one brush after another. So our work must be done. A reform in one line means the readjustment of many things, but we are not to hesitate because to do one work successfully means to attempt many others related to it. The general character of the work must be kept in view, and the duty that comes next must not be overlooked among the many that engage our attention.

God has assigned a task that is ours, that can be performed by being careful of our time and faithful in our efforts. We should bring the idea of preparation up to so high a standard that no one will slight the opportunities for such preparation, and that no one, however well prepared, may dare to rely on himself; but preparation includes the acquisition of the ability to be natural, and when the power of God flows through his people as through inanimate nature, their lives will be both happy and fruitful.

III. Adjustableness in Methods.

Adaptability is as necessary as ability. A wise general disposes his force according to the needs of the moment. One of the obstacles frequently met in Christian work is a love for old plans, which their supporters revere as though they were ordinances of God.

1. *Here the doctrine of limitations and variety must be taught.*—Rain is good, but there are times when it does not fall. The hot sun beating upon vegetation is necessary, but the sun is sometimes behind the clouds. The spring is necessary, but it gives way to summer. The ocean plays an enormous part in the economy of nature, but it has its bounds where its proud waves are stayed. Human life and work are made up of an infinite number of forces, each doing its part to bring about the final result. It is given to no man to do all of any one work. One sows; another reaps.

All this applies in our every-day work. An article of food may be wholesome, if used in moderation, but who would justify a gormand for gorging himself with a solitary viand until he sickened of it? Vivaciousness, in a certain degree, imparts a charm to the life, but how easy it is to cross the line into the realm of foolishness! One must constantly be on the lookout for those points beyond which, if he go, his Christian influence and experience will be impaired. There are limitations to the number of things a Christian may do. It is folly to think one's own sweet will must have its way.

In methods, the doctrine of limitations holds.
Some plans are good in certain conditions, ineffec-
tive in others. An ingredient or two in a method
may be useful, where the entire plan might be
futile.

The doctrine of limitations compels us to accept
the law of variety. When anything fails, something else must take its place. We go from
one thing to another by force of circumstances.
Sometimes, following the laws mentioned, there
must be a return to methods formerly used. Winter clothing is discarded when spring comes, but
resumed when winter returns. So when conditions
require, old plans must be taken up again. This,
too, is nature's method. "Machine methods" are
better than none, but should be provided with an
"eccentric" to adapt to a variety of changing circumstances. A perfect machine is run at the will
of the operator.

We must learn to judge everything, without
prejudice, on its merits. Almost all important in-
ventions, doubtless, had to fight their way against
prejudice. There is a certain amount of superstition in most natures. Old ways should be tested
by the Bible to see whether they are outlined
there; new ways should be similarly tested.

When the so-called "Authorized Version" of the
Bible appeared, one prominent personage said that
he would rather be "pulled to pieces with horses"
than use such a book; and now there are many
who think the Authorized the only correct version
possible! When Jerome issued the Vulgate, it was
not at first generally accepted, but was in fact " re-

ceived with a loud outcry of reproach"; but finally
it was deemed almost sacrilegious to use any other.
Truly, we "build the sepulchres of the prophets,
and our fathers slew them."

There are members of churches, wedded to some
plan acquired by inheritance, who greet proposals
for change "with a loud cry of reproach." Endeavor workers are themselves in danger of
venerating methods that are only a few years or a
few months old, and of viewing propositions for
change with an injured air. We must take heed
lest, after having preached to others, we ourselves
should not be approved.

"*Prove all things; hold fast that which is good,*"
should be the unchangeable motto of the Christian
Endeavor Society. The idea of Christian Endeavor
having been unfolded to the world, many will be
able to develop its details. The original invention
of the locomotive engine has been improved upon
by men who would not have been able to conceive
the original idea. Robert Stephenson would not
be able to manage a modern locomotive; nor could
Robert Raikes direct a modern Sunday-school.

"One plough is better than another plough if it
ploughs better." The practical test is use. A
theory cannot be made to work by insisting that it
ought to work, nor a plan made valueless by refus-
ing to give it a trial. We cannot afford to fondle
a prejudice at the expense of utility.

It is a sad sight to see an able Christian worker
wedded to a custom that has no warrant in God's
Word back of it. Such a match is a "lucifer
match," and causes a fire of contention. On the

other hand, the "new fogy" who insists on changing the old for that which has no recommendation other than that it is new, is as bad as the "old fogy."

Do your duties as they present themselves. Do not try to bend them to a mere theory. There is a logic of facts that is the true logic, when once understood.

2. *The problem of how to put new plans into operation is a formidable one.*—What the worker should do depends on circumstances. If the opposition is only of the nature of indifference, he should proceed with his plans, on the basis that there is nothing to interest others like work actually done. He should not wait to get a general support before beginning.

If he has the legal right to proceed, he should not jeopard his chances by asking the advice of every person he meets. If a man is asked for his opinion, and has none to give, he will probably conjure up one on the spot, and maintain it afterward. The wise worker will set forth his own plan first, if he is satisfied of its feasibility, and will thus win approval from many. If the work is begun, members will fall in with it as a matter of course, and remain its faithful supporters.

The worker should use discretion in obtaining the necessary consent for the line of work proposed. He may not be himself the best person to ask for the privilege, and may need the assistance of some one of known standing. Not unfrequently we must do our work by proxy.

There are opportune moments in a congregation

for starting new plans. Workers should know how to keep their own counsel, and should turn circumstances to account. Often a movement will have to be put on its feet in a gradual way. A little can be done at a time, until the new plan is in operation.

No underhand methods should be employed, but prudence is important. There must not be too much waiting for "logical points of attack." The logical point of attack is the one we can get at.

It is not necessary, in introducing new plans, to speak of all the things that ought to be done, and how you intend to do this or that. Such a speech may raise expectations that you cannot meet. It is better to surprise people by letting them see an improvement here, and another there. People like to see things move, not simply to be told that they are going to move.

Nor need we tear down one work to start another. Old lines can at times be adjusted to new processes.

3. *Besides adjusting the general plans to the necessities of the case in hand, the worker should likewise adjust himself.*—It will not do to presume that we have God's direction in what we plan just because we had it in the last piece of work. David heard the sound in the tops of the mulberry-trees, and defeated the Philistines, but afterward made a serious mistake in his first effort to bring the ark to Jerusalem, and Uzzah paid the penalty of the wrong method with his life.

The parable of the wise and the foolish virgins

teaches that there ought to be reserve power for emergencies. The wise virgins took oil in their vessels, and had wherewith to replenish the lamps which were becoming exhausted owing to the bridegroom's tarrying. The foolish virgins did not anticipate the contingency of the tarrying, or were too indolent to provide for it. We must calculate on times that will try our souls, and not invite failure by lack of preparation. The Saviour carefully taught his disciples to expect trials, that they might not stumble at them. But none should chafe under these warnings, for all may obtain help for triumph in every trial. See Zech. 4:1-6; 11-14.

Prayer for guidance will not always procure an answer through the individual's consciousness. God designs, evidently, that we should be trained not only to pray, but to think deeply and carefully; to use our minds; to read the Bible; to employ every power to know the truth; not to discard thought and expect God to reveal his will in a manner that will contribute to our ease.

He may design to send us to our Christian friends with our needs, to request them to unite their prayers with ours and give counsel, in order to cultivate true fellowship and helpfulness. Again, he may turn us to some well-known principle that ought to settle the matter. In this way Christians learn to observe the fundamental principles of truth—an important ingredient in their thought and life.

IV. The Management of Details.

A Bible school, a Christian Endeavor society, or a church, is like an engine with many parts. A slight difference in the adjustment of the parts makes all the difference in the world in the operation of the whole. In mechanism, extreme nicety is required, and there are measurements down to the thousandth of an inch. In religious work, the best results are obtainable by the most skilful workmanship, and careful thought and investigation pay for themselves many times over. No one would wish for a locomotive engineer a man who knew only enough to manage the throttle, reverse the lever, and apply the air-brakes.

V. Our Fellow Workers.

1. *To remember certain things that relate to our fellow-workers and their work will prevent much unkind criticism, and promote helpfulness.* — Before criticising a worker for lack of success, examine into the facts concerning his work. It may be discovered that he was a hero in his devotion and wise in his efforts. There are battles that rage on with varying fortunes for days before a decisive result is reached. So in Christian work, the weeks of seeming unprogressiveness may really wear out opposing evil.

Perhaps the worker who seems not to grasp the situation may, after all, grasp it perfectly, and the adjustment of his efforts to successive duties may be guided by a keen perception of the immediate needs, as well as of the logical consequences to be reaped.

A conversation with a worker might lead to a revelation of facts and reasons, showing that he had carefully canvassed the subject in all its bearings, and, like a good general or statesman, was planning his campaign far ahead.

2. *In making an estimate of progress* there should be taken into consideration:—

(1). The difficulties that had to be met.

(2). The difficulties that still remain.

(3). The new difficulties that have arisen.

(4). The lines of work that have been successful.

(5). Whether these lines have been followed in their proper order.

(6). Whether what remains has been neglected or is only waiting its appropriate turn.

(7). Whether what has been accomplished is substantial or only showy.

(8). Whether the efforts thus far afford a foundation for future success. This is the chief test. Some are so impatient for a certain feature of success to be realized that they neglect the steps that would make that success permanent.

Sudden development along each line of work may not be expected. God's forces are generally silent. We should be satisfied if our work grows little by little and glides on like the change of seasons. It is evident that everything cannot be perpetually of the marvellous order. God provides quiet hours as well as storms, and calm stretches of water as well as cataracts with their noise and foam. To expect the time of trial as

well as the time of prosperity will prevent un-
mitigated disappointments.

Christian workers are not able to perform prod-
igies constantly. A successful worker, after a
period of excessive toil, may not be able to repeat
the process at once, and others should not expect
it. To sympathize with a worker, do not tell
him you are sorry for his "failure," and thus con-
firm his opinion that he has met with disaster
and weaken his zeal for future efforts, but com-
mend his faithfulness and point out wherein there
have been good results.

[For the subject of Adjustability in Union
Work, see the chapter on "Union Work," under
"Variety in Administration."]

There are ways of putting things that count for
much, either for or against a cause. It is well,
when pointing out a defect, to enumerate evident
good qualities along with it. Sometimes a general
discouragement may result from mourning over
a shortcoming without recognizing the value of
achievements already made, when the exhortation
could have been made in the same breath with a
hallelujah for victories won. A model is found
in the second and third chapters of Revelation, in
the epistles to the seven churches. There, as a
rule, before the reproof or exhortation, a catalogue is given of virtues possessed by the church.
God thus gives all due credit to those whom he
addresses, and we should follow his example.

CHAPTER III.

Under this head will be presented, not a complete compendium of methods, but some of the latest deductions concerning salient phases of the work. Those who wish a complete discussion of methods should consult previous publications, as this volume aims to supply the place of an advanced text-book on the subject.

I. Organization in General.

1. *No Christian Endeavor society can succeed properly without the presence and co-operation of the pastor.*—Pastors who have several churches under their care, and who find it impossible to attend all the meetings of the societies, at least may attend the business meetings of each society, and send brief written communications to the devotional meetings. A pastor with such a charge can hold occasional joint meetings of his Christian Endeavor societies, and present his views.

By his presence in the Endeavor meetings, he will receive inspiration, and will be able to grasp many opportunities to drive home a truth or correct a wrong tendency.

2. *Installation.*—A brief service of installation should be held, such as,—

(1) Remarks by the retiring president, recounting some of the successes of the past year, and suggesting points for improvement.

(2) Remarks by the pastor to the incoming officers, outlining the essentials to success, the responsibilities of officers, etc.

(3) A promise by incoming officers, in concert, to discharge their duties faithfully, trusting in the Lord for strength.

(4) A promise of the members, by rising, to assist the officers in every way, trusting in the Lord for strength.

(5) Remarks by the incoming president, addressed to the society, returning thanks to the retiring officers, and emphasizing the need of co-operation.

(6) These exercises should be conducted by the pastor, and should be interspersed with singing, Scripture reading, and prayer. The whole should conclude with a season of prayer by the society.

3. *A Vice-president of a Christian Endeavor society* should be an assistant president, executing many things that the president plans; not simply a nonentity waiting for a chance to be something. Too often the lines of Oliver Wendell Holmes accurately describe the "vice,"—

> "A vice is something with a screw
> That's made to hold its jaw
> Till some old file has played away
> Upon an ancient saw!"

4. *The Corresponding Secretary.*—The characteristics of a model corresponding secretary are: (1) enthusiasm, (2) system, (3) inventiveness. The

last attribute enables the secretary personally
to solve the problems of the work. Each secretary should make or procure a desk, no matter
how rude in structure, or a section of small boxes,
as a receptacle for correspondence and stationery,
and properly label the departments:—

Calendar.	Stationery.	Ink.
Important Dates.	Stamps.	Pens.

Unanswered Correspondence.	Answered Correspondence.	Business Matters.
		Important Information.

Letters already answered should be retained some
time for reference. Under "Business Matters"
all items to be laid before the society and those
that otherwise pertain to the secretary's duties,
should be kept.

5. *The Recording Secretary* should record more
than business affairs. Other facts pertaining to
the society work should be inserted, that there
may be a connected history of all important matters.

6. *An officer will prove successful as a leader* if,

trusting the Lord for strength and wisdom, he plans work for others, encourages them in the performance of duty, and sets a good example. An officer is not a general in the rear; he is a color-sergeant as well, and must keep the standard well advanced. He must be here, there, and everywhere. He must be official, but not "officious."

7. *The society should have occasions of special interest* in the nature of "rallies," when it will be possible to bring in some who have grown indifferent and secure the attention of others who have never given the work a thought.

8. *Whatever you do in Christian work*, do not regard any one's case as hopeless, though he may be as cold as an icicle. In some instances, individuals may not be reclaimed, and it may not be a profitable employment of our powers to devote to an incorrigible person the efforts that might yield results in some one else; still, we are to hope. There are many who get very low in the Christian life and come up again. This is true of churches also. God's Spirit can work wonders, and we should not despair.

9. *Management vs. Instruction.*—There are workers who deprecate outspokenness, and who believe in "managing things" to bring about the end sought. This plan may be carried too far, and become nothing but the gospel of palaver. When one has been led to an unconscious assent to the plan proposed, his convictions will not necessarily be changed, because he had not been led really to think on the subject. It is generally best to state

the reasons for plans; then those who assent will
do so because they agree with the idea, and can
be depended on in the future to teach others also.
If results are to be secured only by "managing"
people, who will get them to do right when the
"manager" is absent? If religious hypnotism is
to be practised instead of the method of dealing
with persons as though they had honest minds
that could be reached by argument, the subjects
must be kept in the hypnotic condition, for if
released, they may cause no end of trouble. It
would be easier and better to take pains to teach
people than to scheme on the principle that policy
is the best honesty.

10. *Essays in Devotional Meetings.*—A half-liter-
ary basis is not a correct one for a Christian Endeavor meeting, whose aim ought to be the culti-
vation of the devotional spirit and voluntary participation by all. Sometimes an essay may prove
beneficial, but, ordinarily, well-written essays will
discourage timid members, who feel that they cannot appear to advantage by comparison.

11. *Some societies do not show more progress because* too many of the leading members confine
their participation in the meetings to remarks,
and do not pray enough or use enough Scripture.
They do not depend, as they should, on God and
his Word, but too much on themselves. Other
members are prevented from making remarks by
the superior skill of the leading members too frequently shown in the society meetings.

12. *Endeavorers necessarily absent* from any service should be careful to inform the president or

committee chairman as to the cause of the absence, that they may not be regarded as having lost interest. Unexplained absence encourages the latter assumption. Members should guard their own fair name. To give reasons for absence is often an encouragement to others, because it reveals the fact that the person is in earnest, otherwise he would not take pains to remove all doubt as to his frame of mind.

It is not necessary that the individual should always enter into private details in the explanation. I once ascertained that the absence of a certain young lady from night services was due to the fact that she had been giving special attention to a friend who was most grievously afflicted, there having been in the friend's family two suicides and three funerals in two weeks; yet the young lady had not thought to explain the matter, and there were many who believed she had no interest in the society work.

II. Committee Work.

1. *Developing Efficiency.*—The first step should be, to get a good committee; that is, one in which the members are adapted to one another, and composed, at least partially, of persons of experience. The writer believes that, generally, this may best be secured by the president's appointing the committees, in consultation with the pastor. This plan will ensure a large degree of co-operation with the president on the part of the members, and will decrease the liability to friction in making the appointments. Whenever it seems best to select

the committees by any other method, such as through the report of a nominating committee, or otherwise, the necessity for consulting the pastor will still remain; and it would be better still for him to be a member of the nominating committee.

At the beginning of the term, there should be a meeting of the executive committee, to talk over all the society work. At this meeting, the president should be ready with definite suggestions for the chairmen. Perhaps there is an immediate need in the church or society that should be met—one that would not ordinarily be selected as a natural place of beginning for the committee work. The president should start the committees on that which is of pressing importance, and not expect them just to begin anywhere.

Then the committees should meet separately, and each chairman should divide the work to the other members. Many will execute definite work assigned them who would defer action if compelled to plan for themselves. At these meetings, committee helps may be studied.

Each committee should have a secretary, to gather up a record of the work done by the members, and to write reports. This will leave the chairman free to plan.

No committee should try to do alone all the work that is necessary, but should co-operate with other committees.

In the business meetings there should be consideration of the general condition of the society work as well as of the work of each committee. Sometimes all the parts of a machine may be in place, yet may need adjusting. There should be an effort to interest each committee in the work of every other.

Consider what committee is most necessary for the progress of the work *at the time*, and let the other committees feel their responsibility to assist.

Get a wider and still wider outlook over the work of the church, and try to realize the fact that the committees are not for the purpose of making merely the society a flourishing organization, but for the purpose of advancing the work of the church. Impetus for service will come with a realization of the need.

Confer much with the pastor.

Develop your own spirituality. The better Christians we are, the better committee workers we shall be.

The writer planned in the following way to start some committees to work in his society. He announced an "at home" to the members of the society, and called upon the social committee to help receive. The lookout committee was given names of persons on the roll of the society who were not active, to ask them personally to attend the reception. The committee was also told to work at the reception, to induce members to come to a meeting two nights further on, to listen to an address on methods; and at the latter meeting they were to work to induce members to attend the next regular meeting of the society, when there was to be an installation of officers. The regular midweek church meeting occurred that year on the Fourth of July, and the Christian-citizenship committee was asked to work to induce Christians to come to the prayer meeting, on the ground that it was good patriotism and good piety.

A secret of success in setting committees to work is in *setting them at a duty that is near by and of present importance.* If anything is to be done, find something in it for some committee's attention.

2. *Far-seeing Plans.*—Committees and workers should observe the general principle of having some work on hand whose results are expected months hence, as well as work from which immediate results are expected. Nature keeps in action grand and far-reaching processes, as well as momentary activities. A minister may allow some subjects to revolve slowly in his mind, to be wrought out by and by, while he prepares his ordinary two or three sermons a week. Committees may plan elaborately for events to take place at a distant date, and thus make them complete and effective, while they carry out many informal and intermediate plans. Our work should be like the machinery of a clock; some wheels should move slowly, and others fast; but the fast-moving wheels should impart motion to those which move slowly.

3. *Committee reports should contain:* (1). A statement of the number of times the committee has met, and the number of members attending each meeting. (2). Some account of the work attempted, and how far accomplished by the committee as a whole. (3). A statement whether each member has reported work done individually,

and, in some instances, a *résumé* of such work. (4). Suggestions to the society to enlist co-operation, with a presentation of new work to be attempted. (5). In the event that the committee has failed to be active, there should be a report, also written, explaining all the reasons for such failure.

4. *The most important committee* is determined by the changing conditions of the society work. In many societies the prayer-meeting committee is the most important at the present juncture, for the reason that we have passed the founding era into that of edification. In some cases the prayer meetings are all that could be expected, and the missionary committee thus comes to the front to answer the emphatic demand for an extension of service. In the course of time, the lookout committee may again become the most important.

III. The Prayer Meeting.

1. *A good leader* will have something to fall back upon when the meeting really lags, and will have some idea of how to remove a hindrance and lead the people to the throne of God. He will not sit helplessly, nor dismiss the meeting peremptorily. A minister said that if the members did not take part, he would close the service then and there. But if the members were in the frame to participate, they would not need the meeting so much as if not in the proper frame. The pastor is present to help. If a leader does not know what to do with a cold and indifferent meeting, he is as much of a

failure as the members are, and would better dismiss himself, and let some one else lead.

2. *In preparation*, ideas should be gathered for some time in advance, then there should be a selection from this mass of material of that which it is most desirable to say. The mind will be enriched by this study. The preparation may yield but a single idea that is specially important or applicable, but all this study is not too much if it leads to a fundamental thought. Sometimes nothing may be used that has been prepared, but the previous thought and prayer may fit the mind to receive an impression in the meeting that could not have been received without the preparation.

3. *Appointing Leaders.*—The printing of lists of leaders six months in advance has an occasional advantage, in that it may promote a feeling of responsibility on the part of those thus appointed, and at times excite interest; but there are objections to such a method for constant use.

(1). It provides a temptation to prayer-meeting committees to imagine their work all done because the leaders have been selected.

(2). Conditions may arise that would make it advisable for a certain person to lead at a certain time, and these conditions could not possibly be foreseen. Then, persons who may be in a proper spiritual condition to lead a meeting when the list was printed may not be so when the time arrives later.

(3). It may be desirable to employ some new member or visiting Endeavorer to lead, and other contingencies may arise.

(4). If a list is made out and printed, every failure on the part of leaders to be present will be noticed by the society. Discouragement should not be thus invited.

(5). It is well to appoint leaders a month in advance. Changes in such a plan are not difficult to make, and the leaders are thus given opportunity for study and observation.

4. *Intermissions or None.*—The old theory that there should be an intermission of ten or fifteen minutes between the Endeavor and the preaching service is not generally useful in practice.

(1). An intermission furnishes opportunity for some members to pass out unnoticed and absent themselves from the evening preaching service.

(2). Some who do remain indulge in unprofitable conversation through the intermission. The good of the meeting is thus in danger of being dissipated.

(3). Persons are not likely to come into the preaching service in case the Endeavor meetings are held in the same room, and there is confusion.

(4). There is little opportunity for Endeavorers who habitually attend church to induce other Endeavorers to stay, on account of the length of the intermission; but if the preaching service followed immediately, it would be an easy matter to say, "Let us remain for the preaching service."

(5). If the Endeavor service continues till the time of the preaching service, many older members of the church will come ten or fifteen minutes before the preaching hour, and spend it in the Endeavor meeting. This will interest them in the methods, and will also encourage the members; but such persons are not likely to come if they find nothing but an intermission. The plan of an intermission, then, in a measure, prevents the very things the society should try to accomplish; viz., the interesting of members in the church-work, and the interesting of the older members of the church in the society and in more aggressive work.

IV. Lookout Work.

The lookout committee should lead members into the society, and endeavor to secure regular attendance; the prayer-meeting committee should aim to develop the members thus brought in. Division of labor is here a necessity. The lookout committee should "keep tab" on attendance, and the prayer-meeting committee on participation, and each chairman should assist the other.

The question has been asked, " *How shall we remind Endeavorers who have been unfaithful to the consecration meeting?*" Begin reminding them when the first evidences of a disposition to grow indifferent to *any part* of the society work are discovered. The faithlessness to the consecration meeting may have begun far back. The lookout committee should watch *tendencies*. The committee's motto may well be that of the lady who instructed the child in darning stockings, "Mend the holes, and look after the thin places." Failure should be forestalled by constant attention. No member should stand still in his Christian life. When he neglects *any* service, he should be helped

back to the right way. Neglect of the consecration
service means that the case is becoming bad indeed.
An unfaithful person should be brought closer to
Christ, that he may be brought back to his duty.
If he cannot be brought back to the society directly,
he may be interested in some other line of church
work, and thus led to the point of interest in the
society again. If the lookout committee cannot
reach him, some one may be found who can. Pray
for him, at all events. Every lookout committee
should pray.

There is no reason why members should not be
expected to send something to be read at every
society meeting they cannot attend, and not
merely to the consecration meeting, as the pledge
requires.

V. The "Run-Down" Society.

One of the most important questions is, how
to restore to efficiency a society that has lost its
zeal. The subject is a large one, and the suggestions here given might appropriately become heads
of chapters in a lengthy discussion.

1. Ascertain the cause of the decadence, and remove it. In general, the causes are neglect, spiritual drought, local hindrances.

2. Have private meetings of the members who
are interested, and make a salvage corps out of
them. Save the things that remain. Such meetings will prove seasons of refreshing.

3. Assist any line of work in the church that
affords opportunity for growth, and it will confer
a reflex benefit on the society.

4. Do all the good you can in small ways while working at the main idea.

5. Seek to inculcate a wider view of Christian work, and show the field that lies beyond.

6. Send members to Endeavor and other Christian conventions.

7. Turn to your church, like a child to its parent, and say, "Help me!"

8. Get assistance from other societies or Endeavor workers.

9. Labor to save souls.

10. Persevere in doing your own duty. Constant performance of duty in discouraging circumstances becomes, by and by, an example that brings others to a sense of obligation.

11. Do not be content with partial results; seek the highest efficiency.

12. Leaven all with trust in God, and pray earnestly. Grace may lift some of the worst broken-down societies to the highest plane of usefulness.

VI. The Business Meeting.

1. *A General Diagnosis.*—In Endeavor business meetings, aside from the committee reports, there should be, from time to time, essays or addresses on the general state of the society or on some one general present need. It will be readily seen, upon reflection, that committee reports are only piece-meal, and that the general scope and condition of the society's work should receive attention. A doctor tests the pulse, the lungs, the temperature, etc., in order that he may combine the results in a diagnosis; so the society should be studied from

an examination of its various operations. Sometimes an indefinable something seems to be wrong, although the committee reports may be encouraging. The spiritual tone may be disappointing from some cause, or seeds of harm may have been planted in some unknown way. Such matters should come prominently before the meeting. The president may take this general theme on one occasion, the pastor on another, some observing church-member outside the society on another, and so on. This idea is a natural development of our Endeavor work.

2. *To build up the meeting*, plan for a special programme, and use more than ordinary diligence to procure the attendance of members; also invite young people not members, and members of the church who are not Endeavorers. This programme, aside from the ordinary devotional exercises, may consist of the following parts: (1.) Reading of texts on business, distributed to members by the president. (2.) A paper on the business meeting. This should give (a) the purpose of the business meeting, and show that it is a method meeting, to discuss the work of the society, and not merely for routine matters; (b) the relation of the meeting to the success of the society; (c) the value to the individual member in promoting system in his work; (d) the benefit to the church, if the Lord's business were conducted more systematically; (e) our obligation to attend the business meeting, drawn from the pledge, which includes all meetings of the society; (f) how the meeting should be conducted, dwelling upon the

value of promptness, pointedness, etc., in its conduct, with suggestions as to the preparation of committee reports. (3.) This should be followed by brief testimonies from the floor as to the value of the business meeting. (4.) The regular committee reports should follow, each chairman having taken special pains with his report, in this instance. (5.) The discussions and all the rest of the business should be conducted according to the suggestions of the paper, and the meeting should close promptly. A great deal should be condensed into this hour, to demonstrate how it is possible to transact business speedily and properly.

It is not necessary to discuss every committee report at length every month. Such a process is wearisome. The most discussion should be put where the greatest need is.

VII. Sociability.

1. *Care should be taken that society socials* should not absorb to themselves the sociability of the church instead of disseminating sociability through the church. Sociability is like salt, an ingredient, not a separate article of diet.

2. *As to the character of the socials*, it is more clearly demonstrated every year that higher ground should be taken. Deliberately to arrange for that which is light, frivolous, or comic, is an acknowledgment that there is nothing in Christianity itself to produce gladness of heart. Besides, "funny" socials do not promote real sociability; they do not make heart answer to heart. Enough of the witty and humorous will spring up

impromptu. A natural flow of spirit may be wholesome. Young people are not essentially vapid. Many of them *can* be caught with humor, because it has been ministered to them so constantly that they have been spoiled by the lazy method. The old plan simply means, "Produce a vitiated taste, and then cater to it." If the attempt is made to turn to the substantial, after such a wrong beginning, there will then be a new generation of young people on hand, and the old process must be kept up for their sakes; so the round of hilariousness will go on forever.

Instead of cultivating these exterior things to win the young, we should have something in ourselves that will attract them—a wealth of good nature, of earnestness, of sincerity.

If we love them, they will love us. A warm heart, nobility of life, and interest in them will win. They are bundles of sympathy. Be sympathetic also. Pray for them. Do not dally with methods that aim to save them by and by. Go to them with the "to-day" of Scripture, and the "harden not your heart." Do not follow a plan because some good results have been traced to it. There may be a method twice as good. Many plans often employed with some success have their dangers, yet the promoters of the plans pronounce other people narrow because they would avoid these dangers. It is time to fit ourselves for more tactful work, harder, possibly, but richer in results, and more lasting.

Babies need milk; but it should be real milk, containing all the ingredients of solid food, albuminous, oleaginous, and saccharine substances, and not chalk and water.

At least as much care should be taken to create a taste for the lofty in the realm of social enjoyment as to "finish" young people in music, art, or a liberal education.

VIII. The Consecration Meeting.

1. *Training in Consecration.*—One thing needed in our Christian Endeavor societies, and indeed in all our church-work, is training in the idea of consecration—in the proper conception of the word. The following line of topics would make a good evening's programme, or one of the topics might be taken each evening for a month: (1.) True consecration. (2.) How produce it? (3.) How apply it? (4.) How conduct a consecration meeting?

After the first topic has been considered, and all are brought to contemplate the really consecrated life, it will not be so hard to expand the second topic, for it will have been partly answered. Certain ways of producing consecration in others are: A personal life and conduct whose very contact will make them desire to be better; reverence in religious services and after the services; prayer; the use of Bible texts (Rom. 12); training in the idea of consecration.

The third topic is important, for consecration ought to be applied to the committees in their work, and to the whole work of the officers. It must not be an abstraction.

Under the fourth head, many suggestions might be made by way of variety; but if the first three topics bear good fruit, the meetings will be full of power, and power furnishes its own variety.

2. *Varying the Consecration Meeting.*—The roll-call at consecration should usually be followed, for these reasons: (1.) It saves time. (2.) It furnishes an incentive to members to be present by exposing their absence. (3.) It helps to participation by its implied demand on the individual. (4.) It gives to the world a testimony of pledged service by every person whose name is called, and helps to make the members more careful in their lives. (5.) It procures for delinquents the active assistance of others to bring them back to the right way.

3. Still, the calling of the roll may become formal, though personally I have never found it so. However, *it is well to vary the programme* of the consecration meeting occasionally in some one of the following ways: (1.) Announce at the beginning of the meeting that, after a certain point in the service, the names of the members who have not up to that time taken part will be called. (2.) Have the members of each committee rise, when the committee is called, and remain standing until every member has responded; all may then unite in a verse of Scripture proposed by the leader. (3.) There are times when an address on the subject of consecration, defining its meaning, and outlining methods for its development, should be a feature of the service. This may bring all hearts into the frame of consecration, with the result of deepening the meaning of every utterance by the members. By "address" is meant not a

long discourse, but a connected presentation of the
theme, suggestive in character, and brief enough
to be retained in the memory of the hearers.
(4.) On those occasions when, notwithstanding
well-laid plans, the hour comes to a close without
all having had opportunity to participate individually, the consecration service may be continued
to the next meeting of the society; and, besides,
all should be exhorted not to let their good
thoughts spoil for want of utterance, but, in private conversations with others, to tell what is on
the heart, and to undertake at once the duties that
are presented.   (5.) Aside from the regular consecration meetings, there will be times, in society
meetings and conventions, as well as in informal
gatherings and early morning prayer meetings,
when it will seem advisable to conduct a brief consecration service, where the usual method is
clearly out of the question.   In such cases, consecrations may be made *en masse*, or be limited to a
single line of thought most in keeping with the
spirit of the hour, or participation may be confined to a few.

(See "Convention Consecration Meetings," under "Union Work.")

IX. Bible-Study.

This subject is too extensive to be comprehen-
sively outlined here, and is growing every day
more important as a factor in Christian Endeavor
work.   The Bible teaches principles, as well as
specific truths, and we are to make evident applications to particular cases.   To know how to make

a beginning in interesting the society in this department is an attainment to be anxiously sought. Aside from comprehensive systems of Bible-study by classes and in correspondence schools, there are several distinct methods that may be employed in the society to promote the systematic study of the Word of God.

1. *If there is a lack of quotation of Scripture* in the services, call attention to the fact, and ask for more participation by the use of texts.

2. *Appoint a temporary committee*, called the "Bible-study committee," to promote an interest in Bible-study.

3. *At the socials, give Bible test questions*, taking care not to make them too difficult. Such an exercise will be both interesting and profitable. Alphabetical drills on persons, places, and texts will stimulate a desire for further knowledge.

4. *Occasionally have a competent person* give a talk on a general method of Bible-study, or ask your pastor to preach upon the subject.

5. *Get the members to purchase* books containing normal courses. They can be procured at small expense.

6. *If you can*, organize a "Workers' Bible Training-Class." (See "Personal Work.")

X. Junior Work.

For full discussion of this subject, the reader is referred to "The Junior Manual," by Amos R. Wells, the present purpose being but to suggest some fundamental ideas. The qualification of a Junior superintendent is not so much a love of children as a love of truth. The former may be cultivated, if the latter is possessed. From the latter to the former is a short road.

1. *The Benefits of Junior Work.*—Junior work is necessary because (1) It affords such an opportunity to instruct and train as is not found in the Young People's society, the latter society devoting itself more to developing the power of voluntary participation. Junior methods are more catechetical and primary, and revive the useful plan of question and answer so beneficial to the church in past days, somewhat as the Christian Endeavor society presents in new form the class-meeting idea.

(2). The Junior meeting creates an appetite for better things, and promotes familiarity with doctrines stated in simplified form.

(3). It introduces the members into the field of Christian usefulness by training in simple duties, as a father trains his child in easy tasks to familiarize him with the tools he must afterward use.

(4). It instils principles of action, which become part of the life and make it easy for the possessor to do right and hard to do wrong.

(5). It crystallizes good tendencies into habits.

(6). It promotes regularity and system in work.

(7). It creates early a sense of responsibility, thus causing the child to regard himself as of some account in the world, and deterring him from wasting his opportunities.

(8). It opens the gate of the future, and impels to action through a sense of coming possibilities.

(9). It provides, by and by, a trained church.

Timothy, the type, was trained from his youth through the faith of his mother, Eunice, and his grandmother, Lois.

2. *The duty of promoting Junior work.*—Both young and old have a duty toward the Juniors, and should be interested in their work. Would not Christians have rejoiced, in their youth, if there had been a society similar to the Junior society of to-day? Ought they not, then, to promote the work of the Juniors, recognizing thus its value? Do they not desire the Christian Endeavor movement to progress in efficiency as the years pass? Then they should do all in their power to build up from the foundation a better membership for days to come. Love for the Christian Endeavor movement and love for the church both demand interest in the work of the Juniors. The young people will be blessed in their own immediate efforts by such co-operation. A spirit of mutual helpfulness will be generated, and an enthusiasm that cannot exist while the departments of church-work are separated. We speak of the value of fellowship. Should we then neglect it in our own congregations and in our own work?

Some adults will remember that, when they were in the lower departments of the public schools, they looked with longing toward the higher departments, and with almost awe upon the scholars in those grades, and counted it a special honor to be noticed by one of them. But the upper scholars usually have little thought for those below. So the Juniors would be encouraged and helped by attention from the young people; but the young people, as a body, bestow little thought upon them. In every society are many members who theoretically approve, but do nothing for this branch of the work.

3. *Methods.*—(1). The Junior committee should divide their labors so as to compass the various departments of the work, but should still act as a unit under the lead of the chairman or superintendent.

(2). Reports should be made at the business meetings of the Christian Endeavor society, to interest the members of the older organization.

(3). The committee should have at least one young man in its membership. There is no question but that boys can be more readily induced to attend a meeting where there is an efficient male worker.

(4). The Juniors should be taught what it means to belong to the society; the wide purpose of the organization should be shown.

(5). They should be taught how to study the topics and daily readings by examples given in the meetings.

(6). There should be no vacation in the summer.

(7). They should be given simple work, as well as instruction.

XI. Intermediate Societies.

Christian Endeavor has moved on from a boys' and girls' society, as at the first, to rather an adult organization. It is now urged by some of our most prominent Endeavorers that Intermediate

societies be formed, between the Junior and the
Young People's, to care for a neglected class.
Undoubtedly, there are churches in which boys
and girls of from twelve to sixteen are overlooked;
and, where this is the case, one of two things
should be done: either make special efforts to
interest them in the Young People's society, or
organize an Intermediate society. Such a society
should be conducted in a manner between that of a
Junior and a Young People's society. Personally,
I have found it possible to manage all ages in one
meeting; but whatever is best, should be done.

XII. Senior Endeavor.

1. *Senior Endeavor is especially designed* for
older members of the Young People's society,
whose duties render it inadvisable that they
should remain in connection with the latter organization. There is no purpose in the Endeavor
movement to separate the membership into a
series of communities, to the injury of the family
idea, but rather to provide a method of sufficient
elasticity to meet the needs and changing circumstances of growth. The Endeavor society has
"aged" somewhat, and now numbers in its membership many persons of mature years, some of
whom have acquired such an interest in the general work of the church that they have little time
for the performance of duties essential to the
development of the society. It is better that such
should give way to those of younger years, who
need training to fit them likewise for a wide
career of usefulness.

It would be a misfortune if the organization of Senior societies were to result in an exodus from the Young People's societies of all persons of mature years and experience; but the opening of a door of egress might result in such a change in the constitution of the society as would retain only those older persons whose habits, feelings, and methods of work would result in the actual training of the rest. For older members to remain in the Young People's society, doing the formal work, to the deprivation of young hearts and hands, and at the same time not maintaining the attitude calculated to develop the interest and skill of young Christians, is of the nature of the "letter that killeth," and not of the spirit that maketh alive.

The Senior "society" is hardly a society, needing no president except the pastor, and no committee except the lookout. Other committees may be added, but practically the society is only a method to help the midweek prayer meeting, and to lead up to more vigorous service along the lines generally recognized, without a cumbersome organization; for it would be cumbersome if all Endeavor methods were to be applied to the Senior work.

2. *Young people* who desire to take up, avowedly, any additional duties described in the Senior pledge should not join the Senior society for that purpose, but add the items to the pledge they have already made.

3. *The classes of persons eligible for membership* in the Senior society are: (1.) Honorary (affiliated) members of the Y. P. S. C. E.; (2.) Older members

of the Young People's society, such as described in the first paragraph of this article; (3.) Members of the church, not Endeavorers, who habitually attend the midweek prayer meeting; (4.) Members of the church, not Endeavorers, who do not attend the midweek service, but who might be induced to through lookout-committee work. Judging from the benefit derived from the introduction of the pledge and Endeavor methods among the young people, we should expect excellent results by applying the plan to the older members of the church.

XIII. Associate Members.

In an Endeavor convention, the question was asked whether "toughs" should be admitted as associate members. This question reveals a popular misapprehension with regard to the purpose of associate membership. The answer given was: "You are first to try to bring persons to Christ. If you do not succeed, then ask them to become associate members with a view to becoming Christians. One who comes into the society for such a purpose ceases to be a 'tough' at that moment, no matter what he was before. Persons are not to be asked to become associates unless an attempt has first been made to bring them to Christ, for, to such, associate membership would mean nothing." Yet in many cases, doubtless, associates are gathered in from all sources, and then are neglected; and with such a method of recruiting, "toughs" are very likely to be asked to join by persons whose zeal outruns their knowledge of the work.

CHAPTER IV.

UNION WORK.

The proper direction of the Endeavor movement as a whole and in its larger component parts is a problem that transcends almost every other. Prayer for the movement is necessary, that no mistakes may be made in the general work to destroy or neutralize its effectiveness. Not merely as individuals, but in their collective operations, Endeavorers must trust in the Lord for strength.

I. Variety in Administration.

As we ascend from the society to the local, county, State or Provincial, international, and World's unions, the method of administration must change. *In union work we see the need for ripe wisdom now as never before.*

Local and county unions can be managed somewhat after the style of the individual society, but State and Provincial unions must follow in a measure the plan of the United Society. One of the dangers of the movement is, that some may seek to reduce the whole system to an artificial and impractical similarity, not studying that variety which is everywhere exhibited in nature. They would try to manage the large as they do the small, and the details would be cumbersome. It would be like a world all of whose vegetation consisted of oak-trees of various sizes or of flower-stalks of different magnitude, with Virginia creepers three feet thick, and buttercups that held a hogshead. To direct each department with respect to its evident relations, is the true method.

II. Officers.

1. *The selection of union officers* requires thought, experience, and prayer. It should not be made at haphazard, nor be quickly disposed of unless the case is absolutely plain. A duty devolves upon the old and efficient leader to consent to remain at his post, no matter at what cost of time and energy, until the proper successor is found. When a change becomes necessary, diligent search should be made to find the right person for the place.

As a rule, newcomers should not be elevated to places of responsibility. "Lay hands suddenly on no man" (1 Tim. 5 : 22).

Character, judgment, knowledge, and executive force are necessary characteristics. One of the conspicuous present dangers is from theorizers whose minds have not the leaven of practical experience. No one is qualified to direct who does not have horizon. This he must obtain by a great amount of laborious climbing and a patient mastery of details. One must know by previous experience how to judge the hidden features of the landscape, how to trace a river by a line of trees, and how to compute population invisible from his standpoint. Practical knowledge, not local pride or denominational interest, must determine the

selection. Momentary honor will not atone for
the injury wrought to a body of Christians by one
of their number at the head of the work who proves
to be incompetent for the position. It would be
better for them if some broad and fair-minded
member of another body held the place. There is
no real unity, if mechanical exactness must be observed in order to preserve it.

" A workman that needeth not to be ashamed "
is something more than an apprentice. His knowledge is technical. He who is thus skilled knows
how to appreciate and admire plans and suggestions that others pass without notice, as a machin-
ist stands enraptured over the working of some
device that another might not glance at a second
time.

Otherwise discreet Endeavorers may make mistakes in the matter of selecting officers through
lack of comprehension of the movement as a
whole. A gentleman was recommended for a State
presidency, and when his qualifications were in-
quired after, it was replied that he had been president of a branch of a city union! Whether he had
made a successful president was not in evidence;
whether he was a safe counsellor, or well informed
in details, or had organizing ability in handling
large interests, or had even a type of mind that
could grasp the greater ideas of the work, did not
appear. The one making the suggestion had
duties of a kind that prevented him from seeing
the general trend of the movement and the crises
that might arise.

Not only should the best persons be placed in office,

but each should be given the place best suited to his abilities; for every one has his limitations.

The election of officers should be after nomination by a competent committee. Nominations from the floor afford opportunities for the proposal of names of unsuitable persons. The election should not be based on a previous campaign inaugurated by societies or individuals ambitious for local distinctions; and all "booming" methods should be severely discountenanced, as threatening the foundations of things. Sometimes plans are employed to secure a convention that savor too much of the hustings.

2. *Division of Official Duties.*—There should not be two heads to any organization. The president should attend to all duties of an executive character, and the secretary only to duties of a clerical character. The man in the clerk's office of a steamer should not take turns at the wheel. He may know all about figures, but nothing about navigation. In those cases where the president is inefficient, and the secretary efficient, as an executive officer, the latter may assist the former, but the rule should be as stated. Many are excellently qualified for clerical work, having devoted to it all the energy they could seize from other duties, who have, therefore, no time left for the study of the wide movement.

People like to serve under a genuine commander. The passengers on a vessel feel safe if the captain acts as though he were captain and allows no one on "the bridge" but himself; and the crew will love him, for they will see that he is but doing his duty. If he must be stern, still it is better to have a collision with one's own men than a collision with another vessel.

The president should not issue his appeals directly to the members, in all instances; but, as a general would send down his orders to his corps or division commanders, so *the president should communicate with those next him in official position*, and they with their helpers, and so on. It will cultivate a feeling of responsibility on the part of the various officers, when each one is held responsible for the efficiency of his department.

A second important principle is that of allowing some latitude to subordinate officers in the management of details. A general who is too explicit may hinder the efficiency of his field marshals when in the actual presence of the enemy, by preventing them from adapting themselves to the new conditions that may arise. Also, some incentive must be given to individuals to solve difficulties.

3. *Tenure of Office.*—It would be a mistake, in Christian Endeavor State, Provincial, and local unions, to limit the tenure of office to one or two terms. The larger the body presided over, and the more extensive the interests involved, the longer the time required for the incumbent to fill the full measure of his usefulness. Some opportunity must be allowed for experiment, and for the development of plans and the study of results.

Yet it is a mistake for an officer to remain in an office year after year when he has performed a well-rounded service, and has put into it the flower of his energy and skill. It is almost impossible, after years of such constant effort as these positions require, that there should not be some diminution of the energy or some loss of the interest felt in the earlier stages of the work. A new man, carefully instructed by his predecessor, would bring into play new energy, though he might lack in experience. The latter may be supplied by frequent demands upon those who have gone before him.

It is also true that a man's own spiritual interests are likely to suffer from the constant demands of administrative work. He cannot dwell in the constant whirl of public life and yet have that amount of soul-quiet necessary to growth in grace. The performance of outward duty must not bear too large a ratio to inward communion with the Source of power.

It is proper, besides, that other persons should be enlisted in service, not only because there is a certain use in variety, but because it is fair to give opportunity to our fellows to develop and use their ability in a wide field.

III. Conventions.

1. *The Programme.*—The programme of a convention should not be a collection of curios or full of all imaginable things. An artist who would paint everything he could think of in one picture would hardly be considered true to nature. It is better that each programme should have a dominant line of thought, and be arranged according to a defined plan. This will not prevent consideration of those detached matters which are of present and pressing importance. Even these may fre-

quently be grouped with others under some appropriate head, and thus contribute to the harmony of the whole, as well as emphasize the importance of the items thus arranged.

It is difficult to achieve this result if the preparation of the programme is left to the last moment, or if it is made to consist of the indiscriminate suggestions of a number of people. With information gathered from the whole field, and fused by constant thinking and observation, the line of subjects will develop, through a growing apprehension of the needs of the work. As soon as one convention has been held, the work of planning for the next should begin. The president may be supposed to have final authority in shaping the programme, since there must always be last adjustments and finishing touches and unforeseen exigencies to meet; but if he is wise, he will avail himself of every suggestion that comes from a responsible source.

If there is a programme committee, a good plan is for the president to submit such an outline as in his judgment would answer the needs of the work, and ask for comments. At the same time, he should give information concerning the work in the field, and recite the reasons that have led to his suggestions. This will stimulate an interchange of thought, and will tend to unify the ideas of the committee. If there is no programme committee, the president will find it advantageous to consult his executive committee in the same way.

2. *Management.*—Careful preparation is not alone

sufficient to ensure the success of a convention. Skilful direction is to the convention what military field genius is to the battle. Rapid adjustments to meet momentary exigencies and to seize favorable opportunities are necessary in both.

If some of the suggestions given seem commonplace, it is because their feasibility has been demonstrated on many occasions until they have acquired the character of axioms.

(1.) Executive force and skill are necessary here in *the presiding officer.* Hesitancy, sameness, and timidity are as bad in him as in an orator. One who expects to preside over an assemblage should study the methods of those who are truly "masters of assemblies." He should familiarize himself with the programme, the speakers, the business to be transacted, and the proper parliamentary procedure. An unprepared presiding officer is twice as bad as an unprepared speaker. As a rule, the president should preside, because he may fairly be supposed to possess much of the necessary information and equipment; at any rate, he is inexcusable if uninformed.

If obliged to ask for assistance in presiding, select no untried person for the position, if the convention be important; and stand ready to relieve such temporary officer at a moment's notice, if he is not equal to his task. This can readily be done without causing offence by making the invitation for no particular length of time, but only for the existing emergency.

Before the opening hour, the president should ascertain whether all local arrangements are complete and understood, that nothing relating to external matters may mar the programme. Before each session he should see that every speaker understands fully the limits of his subject and the time allotted, as previously defined. Sometimes speakers are troubled with curious lapses of memory concerning these matters. In short, the president should continue his preparation to the very moment of the assembling of the convention, for certain important matters cannot receive their finishing touches till that time.

(2.) Endeavor conventions are not deliberative assemblies, therefore only those *items of business* that are of the first importance should come before the body; the rest may properly be left to the executive committee. The reading of the minutes and other tiresome matters ought not to have a place.

To prevent the proposal of measures that would cause unprofitable discussion, the convention committees should be appointed from the membership of the executive committee, or should report to that committee before reporting to the convention. This will ensure a proper consideration of all questions by those most competent to decide. The interests of the work must not be jeoparded by the often hasty and imperfect work of haphazard committees.

Moreover, all business should be got out of the way before the closing session, so as not to mar its devotional spirit.

(3.) The machinery of the convention, or *the directing of the exercises*, should be as nearly noiseless as possible. There should be a signal code between the chairman and ushers with reference to opening and closing doors, ventilating, distributing bulletins, etc.

The following is a sample of a card of instructions given out by the head usher of one of our State conventions. There was one division of ushers for the day, another for the night.

> Report at rear, middle aisle, on main floor each afternoon at .....; each evening at .....
>
> You will have charge of .... side of aisle No. .... on main floor.
>
> Section ...., Balcony.
>
> Main floor is reserved for delegates.
>
> Placards are on REAR of sections to be occupied by delegations.
>
> Balconies are reserved for ....
>
> Seat no one during prayer or speaking.
>
> Keep the aisles clear, and assist in keeping the hall quiet.

Instead of routine announcements from the rostrum frequently repeated, bulletins may be issued containing printed information, or a bulletin-board may be used and attention called to it by the chairman.

The better a convention is managed, the less it will seem to be managed, like an ocean steamer, which seems to "run herself," though we know that here and there are silent workers guarding every movement. In the very opening session, the Endeavorers should be made to feel that there are many things the Lord would like to have them do; that the convention has only begun, and is not yet made; and that its success depends on individual co-operation. The presiding officer should ask the attendants to study their programmes, and he may occasionally interject a few words to explain the line of thought, but should not waste time repeating what every one can read, nor introduce every speaker with a series of remarks.

Promptness is an essential. Topics should not be crowded over to the next session. It is better to leave out a subject than cause the programme to become congested toward the close. On no account, grant this or that person "a few minutes of the convention's time" to speak on some subject not on the programme. Such addresses should be as rare as angels' visits.

Advantage should be taken of all those tendencies in the convention that lead toward a deeper spirituality or more active service; they should be developed as a wise general encourages the ardor of his troops. Seek for an increase of power and interest as the sessions proceed, and remember that the last few minutes may, by God's blessing, be made to correct the weaknesses of a poor convention, or sanctify the success of a strong one. Guard against the danger of an immediate letting down of the convention spirit, or of an insidious trust in it.

3. *Convention Consecration Services.*—A frequent mistake in consecration meetings at the close of conventions is in making them too long, or rather in imagining that they must be long enough for a great many to take part individually, or for a

kind of complete programme. A convention consecration service does not need to be rounded out as other parts of the programme are; for, if it is, many will conclude that the consecration is now over, and that they may dismiss the subject from their minds. The same is true of some "finished sermons;" they are not persistent in the minds of the hearers. A consecration meeting in a convention and, indeed, anywhere, should open the door to consecration, and aim to send the hearers away with the thought of their need still in the mind. It is like a wise application of a sermon, and applies so closely to the individual's needs that he cannot shake it off. Hence a few minutes spent in bringing the truth home to the heart may be more helpful than an hour spent in going through a mechanical method that is supposed to give everybody a chance to speak. If but few take part with a definite announcement of their intentions, ask all who will seek to know their duty to rise, and turn the consecration meeting into a time of self-examination, which is, after all, a real consecration service. Do not make the mistake of thinking that consecration is in forcing one's self to some kind of a declaration of duty found. There are, it may be, a dozen steps in consecration, and the soul may be led in many ways to surrender itself to God.

A consecration meeting should be spontaneous. I have long since ceased trying to "wake up" the attendants at a convention by urging them to participate. If the meeting is dull, I "wake them up" by calling attention to the evident lack of

the spirit of consecration, and insist that they
take time in prayer in their homes to draw near to
God. Sometimes hesitancy to participate furnishes the text for the leader by which he drives
home the truth. Christians should be taught to
foster the consecration spirit in their closets.
Blessed is that leader who can thus prolong the
season of heart-searching till the hearer lies down
to his rest!

One of the points I usually press is, that "What
wouldst thou have me do?" should be the Endeavorer's prayer. It is vain for one to choose
arbitrarily something he thinks he can do for God,
and then rise and consecrate himself to that.
How does he know that that is the particular
thing God would like him to do at the time?
That is no consecration that does not seek to know
God's will. At times, persons do know what
God's will is respecting them, and may heretofore
have refused to obey. In such cases, the individual may be ready at once with his consecration.

Also, the people should not be taught that one
prayer, breathed on the spur of the moment, may
be sufficient to ascertain God's will, but that God
may say as to Saul of Tarsus, "Go to Damascus,
and it shall be told thee what thou shalt do."
Consecration to *find* God's will may be as far as
some can go at the time.

The writer conducted a consecration meeting in
a State convention, with the subject, "What shall
I render?" and advised the Endeavorers to follow
God's recipe, "I will take the cup of salvation,

and will call upon the name of the Lord." They
were urged to take the promises and opportunities
God offered, and to call upon him for direction;
and the points already emphasized in this section
were presented. The whole service was only
about fifteen minutes long. Those who did not
indicate that they had found their duty, or would
seek it, were told that they ought to spend the
rest of the evening on their knees. "Did you
find your duty?" said a wife to her husband, after
the service, in their home. "No," was the reply,
"but I am on that line. I have never told you,
but it used to be a conviction of my life that I
ought to be a preacher." "But it is impossible
to get you to even talk in prayer meeting, or teach
a class." "Yes; I know that now the only way to
do good is by my example; it is too late for anything
else." But who will say that it was too late? Is
not this method of conducting a convention consecration meeting likely to bear fruit in many lives?
And should we not always aim, no matter how
long or short the meeting may be, to prolong the
power of the meeting into the succeeding hours,
and thus make the good of the convention follow
in the days to come? The convention may be
extended indefinitely by means of the season of
consecration that was merely begun in the convention's closing hours. (See "Consecration,"
under "Special Features" and "Methods.")

4. *Free Accommodations.*—The grace of hospital-
ity should be encouraged. While it is impossible,
in the International Conventions, to accommodate
free of charge those who attend from a distance,

and in most local-union conventions there is no
necessity for such accommodation, yet it is both
desirable and possible in county conventions, and
also, to a certain extent at least, in State and
Provincial conventions. The "pay as you go"
basis would exclude from attendance some who
have insufficient means, but are valuable workers; besides, it affords opportunity for design-
ing persons to make gain out of the Endeavor
gatherings, not giving value received, and neces-
sitates inquiry as to the moral fitness of some
who open their houses for pay. It closes some of
the best homes that would not receive paying
guests, and thus prevents a fellowship that would
be mutually beneficial.

The objection to the free-accommodation plan
is, that it involves a large amount of labor and is
hard to manage. The writer's experience teaches
that it can be made to work admirably. It involves but a careful following of plans that have
been tried and found successful. Too often the
methods employed have been insufficient, and the
efforts not systematic and vigorous. Inexperi-
enced persons may have been placed at the head,
who have not sought information from those who
have learned how to do the work. A few suggestions are appended.

(1). The chief difficulty in obtaining homes for
convention attendants is in the unwillingness of
housewives to remain at home throughout the day
to prepare meals for guests, but they would gladly
give lodging and breakfast; hence it would be
well to limit the free accommodations to the

items named, which would answer the chief demands of the case.

(2). In canvassing for homes, be careful not to ask for "entertainment," but "accommodations"; and call your committee an "accommodation committee." No one desires to be "entertained."

(3). Begin the canvass early, and see that the canvassers understand their duties thoroughly.

(4). If a few days before the convention you are short of places, remember that a final dash at the close may accomplish as much as all the previous effort, especially as at that time a special interest begins to pervade the community.

(5). Information concerning the approaching convention, describing its size, importance, and benefits, disseminated through the press and otherwise, will prove of great assistance. (See convention arrangements, under "State and Provincial Union Work.")

IV. Local and County Unions.

Under the department of "State and Provincial Union Work" are many suggestions that will apply measurably to the work of the county and local union. A local union may be composed of the societies of a city or village or of those of a country district, or of a whole section of a county. The latter may be denominated "branch unions."

1. *A Model Constitution.*—The constitution prepared by the United Society is ample as a basis. Changes are suggested under the heads, "Officers," "Committees," and "Amendments," partly in the phraseology, and partly in the matter.

Officers.

The officers of the union shall be president, vice-president, corresponding secretary, recording secretary, treasurer, and Junior superintendent, who shall be elected to serve one year, and shall hold office until their successors are elected and installed. The presidents of the societies composing the union shall be, *ex-officiis*, vice-presidents of the union during their respective terms of office in the local societies. *The general officers of the union may be installed* by reading to them the constitution, and upon their promise faithfully to perform their duties. An address may also be delivered, outlining the work of the union, and a promise may be taken from the Endeavorers present faithfully to support their officers in the discharge of their duties.

Committees.

1. The officers of the union named in the foregoing article shall be the executive committee, which shall provide for the general interests of the union, and, sitting *ad interim*, may decide upon routine questions left undecided by the convention.

2. A lookout committee of five members shall be appointed by the president, to organize new societies and assist those already organized.

3. Committees such as Christian citizenship, etc., may be appointed from time to time as directed by the union.

Amendments.

Amendments may be made to this constitution by a two-thirds vote of the members present at any regular meeting of the union, provided notice of such amendment shall have been given at a previous convention, or announced by circular to all the societies.

2. *Relation to the State or Provincial Union.*—
County and local union officers should keep the
State or Provincial union informed of all changes
in their territory, and should bring before the
societies all matters pertaining to the general
work in addition to all the State or Province may
do by way of direct correspondence with the
societies.

On the other hand, the State or Province can
nurture the county and local unions by correspondence and through attendance on the conventions
by the general officers. Each State or Provincial
officer, including the vice-presidents, could be assigned a certain district in the neighborhood of
his residence as a field for specific work.

3. *Correspondence with Societies.*—To secure
answers to correspondence, union officers should
use official letter-heads and envelopes; and communications intended for societies should be addressed, not to local secretaries, but *to the society*,
in care of the corresponding secretary, thus:—

To the Christian Endeavor Society
of the............Church,
Care of................, Cor. Sec.,
................,
....

A registration should be taken of all persons attending conventions, to be used for correspondence,
when secretaries fail to reply.

4. *Correspondence Committees.*—The plan of
union correspondence committees, to look after
Endeavorers removing to other localities, has done

much to emphasize the need of this work, but it involves circumlocution. Each society, with the help of the pastor, should follow up its own members. There should be correspondence with the members removing to other localities, and with pastors or churches in the vicinity. The names of pastors and churches can easily be obtained from the year-books of the various Christian bodies, and if there is no church of the persuasion of the Endeavorer, some other may be found of kindred character.

V. State and Provincial Union Work.

1. *The conduct of the business of a State or Provincial union* has been so reduced to a system in one of our older States that a consideration of its rules, with some emendations, is here given. Experience in these matters is the most competent authority.

(1). The president is to conduct all business of an executive character; the secretary's work to be limited to clerical matters; both these officers to be a committee on transportation, the president dividing the duties with the secretary as he sees fit.

(2). The president is to have final arrangement of the programme for the State conventions, using the suggestions of the executive committee as far as practicable.

(3). A State paper is to be the medium for the issuance of bulletins to societies, the publication to be controlled by the State, but no financial obligations to rest upon the union in connection there

with. [County and local-union Endeavor papers
can hardly ever be made a permanent success; and,
besides, the local press affords opportunity for
sufficient announcements and reports of the work;
but State papers, with proper management, may be
made to live, and be widely useful.]

(4). An annual meeting of the State executive
committee is provided for, to be held if practicable, the president to arrange for a public programme in addition to the business sessions.

(5). Current expenses of the union are to be paid
on order of the president and secretary; the treasurer to send an itemized account, with vouchers,
to the State auditor ten days before the State convention, and to present a general statement to the
convention.

(6). The president may fill vacancies in case of
emergency; may appoint vice-presidents for new
denominations coming into the union; and may
delegate some of his own powers temporarily.

(7). The executive committee is to meet at the
State convention, and, in addition to other business, arrange, by subcommittees or otherwise, to
report resolutions, and also to act as a committee
on the place of holding the next convention.

2. *Rules for Local Committees of Arrangements
for State Conventions.*—These rules are also prepared from those adopted by the State in question.
The need of furnishing such committees with
rules has been clearly demonstrated, to prevent
difficulties and delays. Even some of the smaller
details, upon which differences of opinion might
occur, or which might lead to hindrances in the

management, need to be outlined in the light of experience. Some methods that appear most "taking" to a new committee are found not to work well in practice, and would be rejected by the same committee, if they were placed on duty a second time.

(1). The local committee of arrangements is to be organized by selecting chairmen for finance, accommodation, reception, hall, press, printing, decoration, music; also a chairman, vice-chairman, secretary, treasurer, and auditor for the committee of the whole. Each chairman is to have the privilege of selecting other persons to assist him; but these assistants are not to deliberate, but only help to execute plans prepared by the committee of arrangements.

(2). Strict economy is to be observed, and no attempt made to outdo other cities in display.

(3). The accommodation committee is to make it clear to residents that they are expected to furnish only "accommodations,"—that is, food and lodging,—and are not to "entertain" or amuse their guests. [The plan here outlined is advantageous wherever free accommodations in any form prevail, and the method of making assignments will be found useful in all other cases as well.] The accommodation committee is to provide, through the printing committee, a series of cards, to be sent to societies, to be filled out and returned in advance of the convention. [This series provides for those who are to receive free accommodations on certain conditions and for all others. Unions can adapt the series to suit their own needs.] The cards are four in number, each of different color, with general matter, printed in bold type, announcing the convention, time, and place.

Additional information is given on the respective cards according to the purpose of each. The first card is given entire, as a sample; the others in part.

FORM No. 1.   FREE ACCOMMODATIONS.

(Number.)   Convention   *(Name.)*
                    Christian Endeavor Union,
                        (Place and Date.)

M..............................., a member of the Christian Endeavor Society of the .... Church at ....(P. O.), ...(County), has been selected for free accommodations at the State Convention. M .... is alternate.

   Signed, ...
       Corresponding Secretary.

N. B. Your society is entitled to free accommodations *for one person,* provided, (1) you have sent, or will send, by ....*(Date)*........., a report (see blank formerly furnished) to the State Secretary for the year beginning with the close of the last convention; and (2) if the name of the person selected reaches the Chairman of the Accommodation Committee, ...*(Name and Address)*......, by ...., and the free accommodations (for.............) have not been exhausted. Fill out the blank and return to the committee promptly. (See also Form 2.) Assignment cards will not be sent to delegates in advance of the convention. Societies sending in these blanks too late to secure the accommodations named will be informed of the fact.

Form 2 is for "Additional Names for Free Accommodations," and contains, after the heading, the following matter:—

N. B. *If by* ....*(Date)*..............., the free accommodations (for ....), as specified in Form 1, have not all been taken, the additional names, sent in on this form, will be given the remaining accommodations, in the order received *up to* ....*(Date)*.............. Persons who expect to pay their own way, in case there is no free accommodation left, will state, after their names, the rate they can afford to pay, and assignment will be made accordingly. Others will leave the space after the name blank, and if they can be assigned free, they will receive notice.

Then follows space for the names of persons, with the rate per day they wish to pay, and a footnote is subjoined:—

Fill out and return to the chairman of the Accommodation Committee, ...*(Name and Address)*........., as soon as you please; the names will be kept on file till ....*(Date)*..........
If the blank is too small, write the additional names *in ink* on the other side of this card.

Form 3 is for " Credentials." Besides the certificate of credentials, signed by the corresponding secretary, this note is printed at the foot:—

N. B. The bearer will hand these credentials to the Accommodation Committee *in the alphabetical section to which his post-office belongs,* and present the other members of his society. After assignment cards are given, report to the Reception Committee, to be shown the way to your lodgings.

This card also takes the place of registration, and the bearer should see that it contains all the names of those present from his society, and that names of persons who fail to come as expected are cancelled.

If the blank is too small, additional names may be written *in ink* on the other side of this card.

Form 4 is a card of introduction to the host.

All officers of the State union and speakers on the programme are to be given accommodations without further notification.

In the assignment of delegates to their homes, the assignment cards should be made out, with the exception of the name of the delegate, in advance of the convention. Sometimes persons who expect to come do not arrive; and there are also persons who may wish to be assigned together, and if names were inserted on the cards in advance, the committee would be besieged with applications to change assignments. If the name is left blank, the assignment can be made without delay and the wishes met. A number of tables should be provided, and placards prepared for each, such as "A to G," "H to M," etc., so as to separate the delegations according to their post-offices. The lists of names previously sent in should be divided among these tables, with a sufficient number of accommodation cards for each. In the lists thus prepared, the name of the alternate should be written under the name of the principal. [All Christian Endeavor conventions are mass conventions, and the words "principal" and "alternate" refer only to those selected to receive free accommodations. The word "delegate" is a misnomer with reference to an Endeavor convention. . The author has coined the word "conventioner" to describe an attendant on a mass convention.] The process of assignment should be as follows: One member of the committee is to receive the credentials, reading off the name; the second to find the name in the list; and the third to write the name on the accommodation card.

In the case of persons who pay their own way, but apply to the accommodation committee for direction to suitable lodgings, the same process will hold, the cards for pay accommodations being kept separately.

(4). As soon as assigned, conventioners should report to the reception-committee tables, where they will receive a badge, a map of the city, a programme, and be given direction to their lodging-places.

(5). The press committee is to see to advertising the convention, by bulletins sent to newspapers throughout the State three or four months in advance of the convention, and by articles in the local papers; also to provide desks for reporters of both secular and religious papers, but not of Sunday papers, issuing press tickets to reporters, if necessary to admit to the desks.

(6). The printing committee is to have charge of the preparation of badges. If it is necessary to reduce the expense assumed by the local committee, it is suggested that the Endeavorers pay for the badges at a cost not to exceed ten cents each. The selection of the badge is left to the committee of arrangements. The printing committee is also to print the series of accommodation cards, and all necessary placards.

(7). The State union or the local committee, as may be agreed upon in advance, will print the official programme, and distribute it free.

(8). The hall committee is to provide places of assemblage and ushers for the meetings. Churches are the appropriate places for holding conventions, simultaneous meetings being arranged where there is no single auditorium of sufficient size. Some conference will be necessary with the State president in deciding upon the location and number of buildings to be used, and other details of importance. [See paragraph on ushers, under "Management of Conventions."]

(9). The committee on decoration, acting with the local committee of arrangements, is to have full privileges in the selection of the convention colors, etc.

(10). The music committee is to have charge of local musical arrangements, and to provide a choir or choirs to lead the singing. Not more than two numbers of special music at each evening session may be rendered by the choir or soloists or otherwise, as the music committee may decide, the rest of the music of the convention to be congregational, under the direction of the leader selected by the State. All such music will be provided for

in the State programme, in line with the topics of
the convention.

(11). There should also be an information bureau,
post-office, etc.

There are many opportunities for the exercise of
local tact and skill in the arrangements, aside from
the rules enumerated. The development of local
interest is also an important matter. Prayer
should be offered constantly by the local societies
for the State officers, the speakers, and all who are
concerned in the gathering.

3. *Mottoes and Songs.*—Devotional hymns that
recite the purpose of particular countries, States,
or Provinces to extend the kingdom of God within
their bounds are doubtless productive of good, but
compositions that are self-laudatory are not beneficial, especially when they become the fashion,
and result in stale imitation and repetition.
Humorous "cries" and "yells" are not part of
the gospel method, though recitations in concert
of pungent phrases meant to announce great principles or inspire to valiant service have power.
Mottoes and watchwords may be successfully
employed to emphasize present needs, if restricted
to the meeting of important conditions. Not only
in conventions, but on the way to and from them,
there is need for great care, that our "good be not
evil spoken of" through what might appear to
some the substitution of vocal ebullition for devotion. It is true that only incidental criticism may
be made along this line, but so grave are the
interests with which Christians are charged that
they can afford to cultivate only that which is
highest and best.

VI. The United Society.

This body exercises no authority whatever over the local society, levying no taxes or assessments, and conducting no missionary bureau. All efforts to "institutionalize" Christian Endeavor should fail. The genius of the movement and of gospel progress does not permit such a step. The proposition to compose the board of trustees of persons elected by State and Provincial conventions is not practical, because it would give rise to methods of selecting trustees that would keep the Endeavor movement in a ferment; because momentary impulse would often determine the choice where local schemes did not; because the plan would make the board, inferentially, at least, a legislative body, and create a new power in the church and over the church, contrary to all Endeavor principles and to the destruction of the movement. All that is needed is a board void of authority, as at present, to give the movement visibility. There is often nothing more tryannical than a "democracy" wielded by a few determined spirits who use their influence for the incubation of impossible schemes. There is not, and should not be, any authority in Christian Endeavor higher than the church and the denomination.

VII. The World's Union.

This union was formed at the International Convention in Boston, July 13, 1895, and is merely a recognition of the world-wide character of the movement, and has no other standing or authority. It provides for vice-presidents to represent the various lands, States, and Provinces.

PART IV.—APPLICATIONS OF ENDEAVOR.

CHAPTER I.

THE CHURCH.

The church is the agent in proclaiming the gospel; the Christian Endeavor society is a factor in the church s operations. The test of the Endeavorer's faithfulness to his pledge is in his faithfulness to the church. On the other hand, a test of one's faithfulness to the church will be found in his faithfulness in nurturing and building up a righteous and trained membership from the new generations that throng into being. The church is under obligation to train the factors of her progress as the factors are under obligation to contribute all their powers to the church.

A proper conception of the church itself is necessary to the proper application of Endeavor energy to its growth.

I. The Church and Its Mission.

1. *How Established.*—Distinctions are sometimes drawn between the church and the kingdom, as though the church were a temporary expedient. It has been said that the Saviour said very little about the church, but much about the kingdom; but a thorough knowledge of the contents of Scripture shows that the teachers who followed Christ,

to whom the Spirit revealed all things, had little to say about the kingdom, and much about the church, revealing more fully the mind of Christ, and showing that he emphasized the kingdom to impress the character of his reign upon the hearts of men, and organized the church as that kingdom in essence. Moreover, he mentioned both church and kingdom together; and the book of Revelation, the last communication of Christ to man, (Rev. 1:1) was given to encourage and instruct the church (Rev. 1:4, 11, 20; 2:1-29; 3:1-22; 22:16). To understand the mission of the church, all the range of truth should be examined. The analysis must be as thorough as that of a chemist, who knows when he has found all the ingredients of a compound, and does not judge alone by the taste and odor.

2. *All modern methods that would supplant the church* and seek to uplift the masses by means of social philosophy are born, not of expert, but of *ex-parte*, reasoning. God showed the kind of kingdom he wanted by the kind of church to be established. We do not need a new church, but a pure church; not a new gospel, but the whole gospel. The theories of social uplift for the masses, exploited as new, are, so far as they have any real value, but parts of Christianity itself, the practical workings out of the gospel, not the successors of it. Some alarmists who combat the errors of the church will be found only combating errors of their own from which they have just awakened.

There are tendencies to discard the "slow" methods of the church, and, by cheapening the terms, to save society *en masse*. Yet there is nothing cheaper than free grace, and nothing that will bring the triumph of God's kingdom except the work of God's church. Christians have come short of their duty, and Endeavorers should devote all their consecrated ability toward the full assumption of the work committed to the church, and toward working out, on the gospel plan, the salvation of the whole world. "Society" cannot be saved but by saving individuals. Wholesale methods are compromise methods. To realize the perfect ideal for the church is to realize God's ideal for the race. Whatever is done for mankind should be done through the church; the remedy for an inactive church is individual activity in the church. Platitudes are not salvation, nor philanthropy redemption.

3. *Moreover, it is not true that the church is a failure*, though individual members have failed. The book of Revelation shows that centuries of conflict were to come before the triumph of the truth in the world. Shall we then reject the church idea because the church has not gone faster than the prophecies concerning it, because the ground was stony or full of thorns, or because tares were sown in the wheat?

Also, there are moral upheavals now manifesting their power through the work of the church; and a triumph waits at the marriage supper of the Lamb, where the bride of Christ shall be honored before all the universe and in the presence of all the ages.

II. Obligation to the Church.

Obligation arises from the fact that the church is God's agent, and that to serve the church is the most effective way of promoting his glory. It also arises from our own promises made in accepting his salvation. No one can adhere to principle, or keep his word, and neglect the church. No temporary purpose will serve. Individual responsibility faithfully discharged is an element in the success of any congregation. He who neglects his own duty to the church puts a burden on the back of others, and sins against their peace. Church-membership is not for personal comfort, but for active service. We join the church to profess good, or God, to get good from God, to do good for God. It has been well said that the church is "not the pastor's field to work in, but his force to work with." He who misses a service is like a pupil who misses a lesson. The Bible school, the sermon, the Endeavor hour, the prayer meeting, are like a succession of chords in a musical composition.

Obligation demands study of the history of the church, of our particular congregation, and of the world, the church's field.

It demands that we strive to elevate the standard of the church. The higher the standard, the more honor is reflected on those who belong to it, as the standard of a college reflects honor upon its graduates. We may not expect our members to be perfect, but we should expect them to be genuine. A church should have character, the same as an individual. A worldly church is a question mark that casts doubt on all religion. The church should be "first pure, then peaceable."

Obligation demands the development of the heroic. He is not a faithful soldier who fights in skirmishes and minor battles, and is absent when the crisis of a great conflict comes; nor is he a faithful Christian who absents himself from his post when attendance means self-denial. He is not wholly true whose selfish inclinations have their way at critical points. No one makes progress unless he keeps pace with his privileges. A hero is one who performs his just obligations. The world cannot be taken for the Lord by doing only that which is convenient.

Obligation requires that we should promote the unity of the church. A purpose that should run through every action should be to make our work contribute to this end. We should be loyal to the Head; we should love the church, as Christ did, and give ourselves for it.

III. How to Help the Church.

Besides the uplift to the church through the realization of the truths already presented, some of the features of successful church work are:—

1. *The development of the resources* of the Christian by an increasingly systematic study of the Bible, and by prayer—private, family, social, and sanctuary.

2. *The development of personal power and effi-*

ciency by the agency of the Holy Spirit and personal work.

3. *Sociability.* This is Christian helpfulness, not merely politeness. Its special text is Matt. 3: 16; its detailed analysis, 1 Cor. 13.

4. *Organization.* This includes co-operation. The relation of Endeavor work to that of the congregation may be reduced to two maxims,—

(1). *Work with the pastor ;* (2). *Work especially at that which the church needs most.*

CHAPTER II.

The various methods for propagating interest in missions do not demand discussion here, but only the general movement. A study of missions is valuable for the impulse it gives to all our endeavors. It is only as we hear the command, "Go ye into all the world," that we really go any distance in our own locality with a whole heart. Each apostle was called to the task of turning one twelfth of the world upside down. We should be apostolic in our faith, and do our modified portion of the work in the shortest possible time.

1. *The work of the Endeavor society is not to create a missionary bureau* or any new agencies to supplant those already at work, but only to produce enthusiasm to be employed by the various church boards. To this end, nothing should be done that would give weight to the erroneous idea that the Endeavor movement has its own distinctive missionary work. Each denomination might appropriately appoint Endeavor workers to arouse missionary interest among the societies. This would emphasize the fact that Endeavor propagates the work of the denominations, and that each society is taught to be true to its own church.

2. *How to Send Contributions.*—Unless otherwise directed by the denomination, all Christian En-

deavor contributions for whatever board should be sent not only to the board direct, but also through the church treasurer, credit being given to the society. In this way, the young people will be bound more closely to their church work. Otherwise, the societies may come to have a complete schedule of contributions for the whole list of church boards, and thus become "little churches," apart from the congregation. Appeals for money should be made to the church, and the societies asked to help the congregation to raise the amount, credit being given to the societies for the share they take in the work, and for the amounts contributed.

3. *Fundamental ideas* concerning mission work should be inculcated, that methods may bear fruit.

The point to which all Christian work tends is that of the salvation of the world. The society is a component part of the church, and the church exists for the purpose of taking the world for Christ. It requires the same consecration to preach the gospel at home as in foreign lands. To work with all our might demands as much reliance on God in one place as another. If a young person is not impelled to make a consecration of himself for foreign work, he can become consecrated to equally hard work at home, and propagate missions in his own church. No one is fit to preach the gospel in his own land until he is ready to go anywhere. God may bring us to the test of willingness to go to the ends of the earth, but after we have yielded he may keep us in our own coun-

try to ignite others with missionary enthusiasm.
A missionary is one who has a mission, as we all
have, and missionary zeal must characterize our
work at home; for missionary spirit is the same
the world over, and sin is heathenish everywhere.

It has been rightly intimated that the man who
does not believe in foreign missions is the greatest
heretic there is; he does not believe in the Ten
Commandments, the Lord's Prayer, the Apostles'
Creed, or the Doxology.

No one is properly interested in any subject until
he is interested in the statistics of it. Surely, God
would like us to inform ourselves concerning the
facts and figures, and then instruct others. Let
our consecration be, "I will do what he would
like to have me do in this also, and will prepare myself for usefulness along this line." If we
have missionary material in us, we shall show it in
work *for* missions.

The young are especially called upon to be foreign missionaries. They have energy and years for
service, and the millions of young people dying in
heathen lands should appeal to the young at
home.

Mr. Wilder has said that the motto of missions
is, "Your money or your life!" Rather, it is
"Your money *and* your life." No one, in deciding
whether he should go to the foreign field, should
think of possible evil consequences to his own
church through his absence. It did not hurt the
church at Antioch for Barnabas and Saul to be
separated to the work of saving the heathen
world.

Let Endeavorers ask themselves these questions: (1). What have we done to promote systematic and proportionate giving? (2). What methods have we employed to interest our members in missions? (3). What have we done to present the needs of the boards of our denomination?

CHAPTER III.

This subject must always be closely related to that of missions, and it is, besides, one of the important lines of culture in our Endeavor and other church work.

I. Christian Financiering.

1. *Christian beneficence should not be a matter of haphazard, but of careful financiering.* System and thought are as important here as in the United States treasury department, and the same type of financial ability is demanded.

Divine love sits like Lazarus at our gate, begging for crumbs. Giving should be systematic and self-denying; but it should be first *systematic*, for system will lessen the degree of effort, and will thus make it necessary to give larger amounts to experience self-denial. It is not possible to give as we ought by giving spasmodically any more than it is possible to be good by spells. An individual said, "I, too, am sanctified—in spots!" We should not be content with such a sanctification of our beneficence, but should mourn ove. the unsanctified spots.

2. *Liberal and systematic givers enjoy giving.* The Bible says that we should "abound in this

grace also." Giving is therefore not a mere duty, but a grace without which the Christian life is incomplete in character and joy.

3. *Giving is an act of worship.* It should not be denominated "taking up a collection." Footpads and train robbers take up "collections," but Christians make offerings.

4. *Nor should the Christian say when easing his conscience with a small offering,* "I can give you the widow's mite," for the widow's mite *was all she had.* The weak things of the world are to confound the mighty, and the nickel given with self-denial and prayer may confound the dollar given by an evil man for an unholy purpose.

5. *The men at the head of the financial department of the church should be like the first deacons,* "full of the Holy Ghost," not just any men of business who have been prudent in their own worldly transactions. Many are good financiers in worldly matters who do not lay the Lord's business to heart as they do their own, because they are not "full of the Holy Ghost."

6. *In giving, Christians must often be like soldiers in a battle*—forget everything but the paramount interest of the cause, and rush into the breach with an abandon that is an example to all the rest.

7. *Endeavorers have promised to do "whatever the Lord would like* to have them do." In their consecrations henceforth let them realize that God would like to have them systematic and self-denying in giving.

8. *We should plan to have money for the Lord's work,* by curtailing personal expenses, by earning

something for his treasury, by setting apart a portion of our income.

II. Objectionable Methods.

1. *All methods taken in lieu of systematic and proportionate* giving are a delusion, and afford no relief to the church. The more they are resorted to, the more they must be employed, for they create the condition they seek to remove; dependence on them makes further dependence necessary. A church educated along such lines, when poor, will reluctantly depart from the methods in which the members were trained. The employment of unscriptural plans leads to the neglect of others that would have yielded better results.

2. *The means frequently employed are really expensive,* yielding but a slight profit for the labor performed, and are a prolific source of difficulty in the church and of criticism by those outside. On the other hand, scriptural methods yield a rich return, and at the same time build up the spiritual power of the church. How important, then, is it that Endeavorers should make training in systematic beneficence one of their main objects!

III. How to Train in Systematic Giving.

1. Appoint a temporary committee for this line of work.

2. Ascertain how many systematic givers there are already in the society.

3. Give opportunity for the members to consecrate some definite portion of their income to the

Lord. This may be done advantageously at consecration meetings. By income is meant what one
gets for his own use, whether regularly or occasionally. If they will not consecrate a portion for
all time, ask them to do so for a period—a month
or a year; but emphasize the duty of making the
consecration for all time.

4. Let those who have tested the plan testify of
its blessings.

5. Show by comparative statements the value of
the method.

CHAPTER IV.

CHRISTIAN CITIZENSHIP.

I. Need of System in the Work.

1. *The difficulty with much work in the field of moral reform is that it is disjointed, spasmodic, and irregular.* The lawbreaker counts on Christians' giving up the fight. The saloon-keeper can afford, so he thinks, to put down his blinds, close his doors, and counterfeit a law-abiding air for a few weeks, only to resume his wonted career when public sentiment has returned to its normal condition of quiescence or acquiescence. The rogue in office bows for a season before the blast of "whereas" and "resolution," contenting himself with the assurance that all he has to do is to "lie low until this breeze sweeps by."

So thoroughly has this belief in the evanescent character of reform movements ingrained itself in the consciousness of wrong-doers, and in that of the general public as well, that there are many who assert that permanently to overthrow evil is impossible. Acting upon this conception, lawbreakers lay new schemes and plan further trespass.

To neglect system, in the face of such awful need, is crime. We are not to diminish our enthusiasm in order that it may be easily managed, nor dribble it out so that it may be made to go round, but should rather plan for a system adequate for the direction of the largest enthusiasm. Our capabilities for system are as limitless as our capabilities for action.

The forces of evil are systematic, and it is largely by their system and persistence that they succeed.

2. *Enthusiasm should take the direction of disciplining and drilling the forces;* it will make it easier fighting further on. That is not enthusiasm, but effervescence, that is unwilling to take pains in preparation.

In actual warfare there is a continuity of purpose, a swaying back and forth of the armies, like two wrestlers, till one or the other is conquered. One army pushes the other back a pace, and does not then pause to congratulate itself on the point gained, but pushes again and again, until the enemy is overwhelmed in the last ditch.

3. *Some generals do not know what to do with a victory,* nor how to make the most of an advantage. We should know how to seize an opportunity and pursue a flying foe; how to hold a position gained; how to drive the enemy from point to point; when to order a direct assault, and how to repel a bayonet charge. Our system must provide for maintaining the work in a vigorous form, even when the circumstances that give rise to it have passed away. *Eternal vigilance is an attribute of system as system is of true enthusiasm.* Let no one who does not intend that the pulse of his patriotism shall beat regularly enlist in this effort. Christian-citizenship work must be put into the

catalogue along with eating and sleeping and the performance of the daily routine of life.

4. *The work includes not only the reform of existing evils,* but the eradication of evil tendencies and the education of the mass of citizens so that they shall instinctively hate sin and love good. This is a work requiring time; but the worker will be cheered by some immediate results, and faith will reward effort with the confidence of victory. As at the conquest of Jericho, the preachers may carry the trumpets, but the *armed men will go before,* and there will be a rearward to follow!

5. *Public sentiment does not need to be ." educated,"* but to be crystallized. We must work as did the Jews in the days of Nehemiah, with one hand grasping the implement of labor, and the other holding a weapon. We can crystallize sentiment by constant effort in the belief that each effort counts.

6. *Zeal should be tested* by putting it in harness, and purpose should be developed by the aid of perseverance. Self-denial in this field brings rich compensations, as elsewhere.

II. The Plan of Campaign.

Some methods are needed that are applicable to ordinary society work, to interest persons of both sexes, since all have influence. Civic clubs for the study of government are useful, but do not meet the immediate want of the Christian Endeavor societies. The plan of campaign here proposed is threefold.

1. *It is educational.* A study of municipal affairs

and of the general scheme of government can be conducted in the monthly business meetings, in oral drills or otherwise, by the Christian-citizenship committees, in connection with their reports.

Let some competent person prepare an abstract of the laws of the municipality, State, or Province touching important points, and, if possible, publish in the local papers. The whole community may thus become familiar with the laws by which they are governed.

Literature bearing on Christian-citizenship work and moral reforms should be freely distributed.

2. *There should be an investigation of lawlessness and maladministration.* The people should learn not only what the law is, but to what extent it is not kept. Facts will arouse more than speeches.

Literature on this head, concerning the moral condition of the whole country, as well as of the immediate neighborhood, should be disseminated.

3. *There should be a presentation of feasible methods of work*, by which the evils may be corrected.

(1). One of these is a pledge for a voters' federation.

The pledge here given is modelled after the voters' federation pledge of the Ohio Anti-Saloon League. It should be signed in duplicate, the signer retaining one copy. Such a pledge may be made the basis of an organization, whose efforts should be directed by a committee.

Voter's Pledge.

Acknowledging my primary allegiance as a citizen to be to God, humanity, and country, I promise to make my political action conform to these higher claims; and that, to the best of my knowledge, I will vote, in caucuses, primaries, and at the polls, only for persons of moral integrity, who are known to be, and who have avowed themselves to be, opponents of the saloon.

Signed......................

Address.........................

The following "agreement" for a single election has proved effective:—

No. 2,198.

THE MUNICIPAL LEAGUE OF TOLEDO, OHIO.

Voter's Agreement.

I hereby agree, for the approaching spring election (18—), that I will attend the caucus or primary and the general election, and vote only for candidates who are known to be, and who declare themselves to be, in favor of a business management of city affairs and the diligent enforcement of law.

Name............................

No.......St.....................

Ward...........Precinct..............

SIGNER PLEASE CAREFULLY PRESERVE THIS DUPLICATE.

(2). The citizenship committee may assign its members to the chairmanship of subcommittees, as follows:—

The agitation committee to hold public meetings and arrange for scientific lectures, distribution of literature, etc.

The law-enforcement committee, to see to the observance of any existing laws requiring instruction in the common schools on the effects of alcoholics and narcotics; also to secure from the officers of the law, by petition or otherwise, the enforcement of the statutes. [It is not best for citizens personally to enforce the laws, unless, in certain instances, to demonstrate the inefficiency of the officials. Law-enforcement by citizens will tend to make the officers of the law less active.]

The legislative committee, to procure the enactment of better laws.

Then there may be meetings of the various local committees, public addresses, the dissemination of literature, and agitation, agitation, agitation, to arouse and inform the public. There are times, of course, when quiet work is more effective than an open campaign.

In our prayers, the nation, the State, the municipality, the neighborhood, should be remembered. In these civil divisions much of our happiness is bound up. We are careless of our own welfare, if we do not devote time and study to these institutions. Toil here means the salvation of souls, and makes all the rest of our work easier. Bad government tears down what Christians build up, and builds up what Christians would tear down.

These lines of work in a local union may be conducted by a union committee, or, where there is but one society, by that society alone.

(3). Dr. W. F. Crafts, superintendent of the National Reform Bureau, Washington, D. C., suggests certain steps that may be taken in a systematic effort to procure good government, such as: first an appeal to the chief of police or police commissioners; then an appeal to the mayor; next to the sheriff; afterward, to the governor; finally, efforts of citizens to enforce the law and to elect to office men who will enforce the laws.

Something may be accomplished by encouraging officers to do their duty by making them feel that public sentiment will support them.

(4). In organizing a campaign, it is not necessary to make a public parade of the movement, or, indeed, to begin with a mass movement of citizens, though at times there may be such a spontaneous uprising. Experience indicates that all that may ordinarily be necessary is for a few persons to form plans, deliberating in private, and obtaining the co-operation of others along the lines thus determined upon. The community will often follow a movement they see in existence, while too much public debate might result in the movement's being captured by its enemies. Nor is it necessary to mould into one all existing agencies for reform, but all such may co-operate in certain particulars. The more forces in the field, the more the enemy will be confused, if only the friends of reform do not work at cross-purposes.

(5). Though we may not be able to overthrow an evil at once, it may at least be held in check and the consolidation of its adherents prevented, while the friends of righteousness are, at the same time, drawn into solid array. The drawn battle we fight may secure a victory elsewhere for another detachment of the army.

(6). To continue a reform movement after a campaign has been fought, it is probably not best to maintain the organization *en masse* in all its parts, for it is always difficult to keep the interest of a whole community at white heat; but the outlines of an organization may be preserved in the persons of a few faithful workers in each precinct—a sort of standing army which may serve as the nucleus and governing power of a larger host when the time for another struggle arrives.

CHAPTER V.

All true Christian Endeavor culture must tend toward this department of effort. If all Christians were soul-savers, the problems of moral reform and missions would be solved.

I. Preliminary Conditions.

Preparation is necessary to the attainment of proficiency. The world had to be prepared for the coming of Christ; a heart must be prepared; a church must be made ready.

The idea that a church's chief work is the saving of souls is a correct one, but souls can be saved both by individual effort and by erecting in the community an institution of so high a standard of righteousness that it will attract men to Christ. The ordinary work of building up Christians has for its end the salvation of souls. Preaching must not be all evangelistic in the distinct sense; Christians must be led to fuller knowledge as a preparation for work. The building of a hospital takes time, but it is better to build than to trust to individual spontaneity in caring for the sick; so, to train a congregation for service may take longer in getting at a wide work, but it is better for the unsaved in the end. It has been said of the late Dr. Gordon, that he did not prepare sermons, he prepared himself.

There should be an exaltation of the true conception of what it is to be a Christian, as a preparation for saving—not merely arousing—men. Preparation does not consist merely in a longing for a work of grace, but in doing all the good possible and asking direction for higher service. Obedience is the precursor of blessing.

To prepare the way, *there should be a right view of the situation.* The work cannot be done in a day. The devil will match enthusiasm with enthusiasm, skill with skill, and we must draw deeply from the power of the Holy Spirit to succeed.

Straight paths must be made for the feet, and plain, open principles taught. We must make a highway in which the Lord can walk in a manner becoming his character. The Lord will not follow in the path of some churches, avoiding every square issue, concealing every definite opinion. He will not come on the paths which the mountain goats climb, but on a highway, with a train and banners floating before him. A John-the-Baptist method of preparation has not become useless. Old-fashioned repentance is not too hard for the reception of a free and complete salvation.

The church should be made a glowing centre of spirituality, the better to take care of new converts, and not a cold-storage warehouse. A church should have a character for holiness and consistency, so as to be a standing invitation to men to come and be saved.

Soul-saving will promote soul-saving. Every

Christian should be at once diligent to save men; but great preparation is necessary to produce the best, the most numerous, and the most lasting results.

Preparation may be rapidly secured, in certain instances, for God is ready to fit us when we are ready to be fitted.

II. Workers' Training.

Abraham had done much that proved his sincerity before God spoke to him and told him to be "perfect." We are not perfect in anything, either method or conduct, or in any phase of knowledge. Training is the Christian's constant need, his ever-recurring duty. In evangelistic work, persons learn the *a b c* of Christianity, but they must learn how to group these principles into words and phrases of service. After evangelization comes edification. Yet few are really attracted to that which professes to train. Few religious papers contain a department for the training of workers.

The preparation of the individual for service is a deeper work than instruction in method. It is training in the *fundamentals* of life and service.

The response to such effort is slow. Some necessary processes can be placed upon a proper footing only by long and enthusiastic effort. In this line of development there must be pioneers who live ahead of their times and prepare the way for the triumph of the principles involved.

1. *The Acquisition of Courage.*—Granted that the worker already feels a deep responsibility for the salvation of men, and that he has consecrated him-

self to such service, the problem still remains how he may gain sufficient courage to attempt the work. The following considerations may help to produce confidence.

(1). Many of the unconverted are waiting for Christian guidance, and wonder at the tardy efforts. An acquaintance of the author, who is now a Christian worker, waited two years for some one to speak to him about his soul's salvation, and finally, taking the initiative himself, found it necessary to make two or three journeys to find the pastor, to express his desire. Acts 16: 9.

(2). The worker should consider the good wrought by saving a soul. Jas. 5: 20; Luke 15: 7.

(3). He should think of the sin of neglecting a soul and the ruin thus caused. Matt. 25: 45.

(4). No personal injury is likely to result to the worker; and gibes, cold receptions, or rejections are not worthy of consideration. Acts 21: 13.

(5). Anger on the part of the person approached may give way to humility, especially if the worker shows a forbearing spirit. Matt. 21: 28, 29.

(6). Our own salvation was due to some one's personal effort, and we are grateful for the interest shown; and the unsaved will respond to Christian interest as we did. Other workers have succeeded, and why not we ? We should show our love for men by personal work for them. 1 John 4: 21.

(7). Those who have been faithful in soul-saving testify to its joyfulness. Acts 14: 27.

(8). God commands us to do this work, and we

have no right to hesitate; it is a question of simple obedience or disobedience.   Mark 16: 15.

(9).   God will help those who attempt the work. 1 Cor. 3: 9.

(10). Nothing done for God will fail of a good result. Isa. 55: 10, 11.

2. *The Locality of the Work—Highways and By-ways.*—Service must be in season and out of season; that is, when circumstances seem favorable and when they are not; we must sow in the morning and the evening, for we know not "which shall prosper, whether this or that, or whether they both shall be alike good"; we must "begin at Jerusalem"; we must go to the streets and lanes, and then to the highways and hedges; we must work in our own congregation, as well as among the outcasts.

If we went out from a congregation and planted a mission station, that would be going into the highways, but it may still be quite a distance to the hedge in some cases. As we went out from the central church, we must go out from the mission; as we went out to the highway, we must go from thence to the lanes; as we went to the hedge, so we must go to the jungles; as we went to the jungle, we must go from that to the pit. Human souls are lodged in the crevices of sin; they have crawled into the burrows of vice; they are stowed away out of sight in the depths of evil. The personal worker should be ready for any kind of service, not alone for that which is dainty.

3. *The Beginnings of Personal Effort.*—(1). Learning by Doing. The best way to learn a rule is to

follow it. Do as it says, and you will come to understand it. Processes lead to principles. It is a wrong method to try to comprehend the "why" before you have attempted the "how." We acquire skill, as well as understanding, by doing. A theoretical knowledge does not make one successful without practice. In this connection, see John 7: 17, Revised Version.

(2). There must be constant reliance on divine wisdom and grace. The disciples thought they could fish without divine help, but, despite their arts, they caught nothing; they could not get the net down where the fish were. When Jesus gave a word of direction, the net was speedily full.

(3). Principles of Progress.

(a) Begin with the duty that is nearest; it is like a lesson that helps to the comprehension of the next.

(b) If a work seems too hard to accomplish all at once, make at least a beginning—do some of it.

(c) Follow up your last work with further effort. Do not simply make beginnings. Finish something.

(d) Help others in what they are trying to do.

(e) Get help from others in what you are trying to do.

(f) Pray over your failures and be modest about your successes. Ask God to bless what you think you have done well and overrule what you have done ill.

(g) Remember that good comes of every honest effort; hence you need never grow discouraged.

(h) Remember that there is an ingredient of

human weakness in all that you do; hence you ought never to be satisfied.

(*i*) Endeavor to progress in your efforts. When any duty becomes easy, attempt the harder ones just ahead.

(*j*) Do not be too gradual in your progress. Attempting harder duties even before the present one is entirely compassed, will help you to perform that in which you are already engaged.

(*k*) Your own spiritual life must be fed to provide strength for work.

(*l*) The Word of God, prayer, and meditation are the elements on which the soul is nourished.

(4). Steps of Advancement.

(*a*) Be present at all services of the church.

(*b*) Go to mission stations and observe the workers.

(*c*) Shake hands with people you know only slightly; and then with strangers.

(*d*) Distribute notices of meetings, and send leaflets and Scripture cards through the mail.

(*e*) Give personal invitations to attend church services.

(*f*) Call on persons who have lately come into the community.

(*g*) Ask your pastor for names of other persons on whom you may call.

(*h*) Go the first time with some experienced worker.

(*i*) The next time, go alone.

(*j*) If you are discouraged, talk the whole matter over with some one competent to help.

(*k*) Join a Christian Endeavor society and learn to take part in the meetings.

(*l*) Pray for certain individuals, and get others to pray for them.

(*m*) Ask prayers for yourself.

(*n*) Cast out from your life everything that is inconsistent or that may prove a hindrance to your Christian efforts.

(*o*) Systematize your duties so as to have time for Christian work.

(*p*) Study Christ's methods.

(*q*) Study the Bible carefully in its various departments, so as to be ready to give Scripture texts on sin and human need, the plan of atonement, acceptance by faith, Christian life and service, the work of the Holy Spirit, and assurance, and to show the inquirer where to find the texts in the Bible.

4. *Dealing with Inquirers.* (1). *How to approach any one* on the subject of personal religion, is a serious question with most people. There are three general answers to be given.

(*a*). The method of Philip in approaching the Ethiopian chamberlain will cover a great many cases. He yielded to the command of the Spirit of God, and probably had no more method in mind than just to start to catch the chariot as commanded; but the opening sentence, though seemingly abrupt, was the proper one for the occasion. Our duty is to start, and trust God for wisdom in opening the conversation. Many souls are lost for lack of following this method. We must run on God's schedule to connect with opportunity.

(*b*). Seize opportunities which the unconverted themselves present. There are inquirers who, like Nicodemus, will broach the subject of religion. We should make such conversations personal. There are other opportunities which by a very little tact may be made to lead to the general topic of religion, and from that to personal religion.

(*c*). We must make opportunities. This may be the hardest of all; but the handing of a leaflet, the writing of a letter, a visit to the home, may be made means of approach. Usually, the first step is to gain the friendship and confidence of the person. In all cases, a consistent life is an agency in the conversion of others. A good name is an indorsement of the religion of Christ, even as a good name on the back of a check makes it marketable.

The testimony of those who have attempted such service would be, in most cases, " I found it easier than I thought." Religion is not such a tabooed theme, after all, and people are more willing to talk upon the subject of personal piety than is generally supposed. Let us imagine a conversation or two, by way of suggestion as to method.

" Good morning, Mr. D."

" Good morning, Mr. H."

" I have not seen you for a long time."

" It has been over a year, I think."

" How time passes! It seems but a few weeks since we last met."

" Yes, a year is soon gone."

" And each year passes more swiftly than the last."

At this point the conversation may take either of two turns. The person addressed may seek to drop the subject, or he may choose to follow up the thought suggested; but, at any rate, it will be seen how to lead the mind in a given direction. Any one who wishes can direct conversation into a given channel. We may begin with talking politics. It is not necessary to inquire how persons get on *that* theme.

"What do you think of the tariff question?"

"I have no special opinion as to the wisdom of the measure; I am no tariff expert."

"Well, now, my mind is clear. You see," etc.

"That may all be true, but I have been giving my thought to a subject that I consider of vastly greater importance, and I have ideas on that."

"What is that subject?"

"Not the duty the importer pays to the government, but the duty every man owes to God."

"Why, ha! ha! I thought salvation was on the free list!"

"Then why have you not obtained it?"

The directions in general are:—

Talk about religion when you know it is in the person's mind, such as after a sermon, etc.; turn ordinary conversation into religious channels.

(2). *When called to minister to a sick person,* especially one who is supposed to be dying, one of the most difficult of all services, the following method will be found useful.

(*a*). Try to get the person's thought away from himself to God, and keep it there.

(*b*). Calm his mind. Assure him that there is

time enough yet to be saved, for the instant he searches with all his heart (that is, accepts fully) he will obtain salvation. Jer. 29:13; 2 Cor. 6:2.

(c). If you have no text that seems to fit his need specially, give him the one that let light into your own soul, and to whose truth you can give personal testimony.

(d). If any promise seems to reach his heart, tell him to hold to it, and follow its teaching, that it may lead him to God.

(e). If he profess conversion, help him to take up some Christian duty, if it be but to speak to those about him.

(f). It is often best, first of all, to arrange that others may leave the room, that you may be alone with the sick person, as many cannot speak freely in the presence of their friends.

(g). The sick person should be taught to pray for himself.

(h). Aside from specific encouragement, as contained in the promises, the general plan of salvation should be explained.

This process is suited for the most urgent cases; care is needed in the sick-chamber not to excite the sufferer physically. The gospel properly presented will comfort and strengthen.

(3). Following up Opportunities. There are many ways of doing this. One is, simply to press home the truth again and again, remembering that many attempts fail for lack of continued effort. Another is, to interest other Christian workers in the individual, and secure their assistance. In all your work you must make the person feel that you are interested in *him* and that your efforts are not formal.

(4). A Short Course of Instruction. To present to an inquirer the whole subject of conversion, life, and service may often be necessary to his understanding any part of it. The following outline will be useful in such cases.

(*a*). *Conversion.*—This is not a question of extensive knowledge, but of genuine faith. Quote John 3:16. Coming to the Lord consists not only in asking for pardon, but in giving one's self to God. A prayer for salvation alone may be a selfish prayer. Soul-surrender is a necessary part of penitence. We must not only pray to be *saved*, but must offer to *serve*. Having coming honestly and unreservedly, we must believe (John 6:37). To "look" to Christ means to trust him. Conversion includes confession. (Rom. 10:9, 10.)

(*b*). *The Christian Life.*—This is like going to school. If we skip one lesson, the next will be harder; but if we learn each lesson in its place, and master each rule in turn, working out all the hard as well as the easy problems, progress will be natural, and we shall enjoy the work. We can get daily grace for daily needs.

(*c*). *Relation to the Church.*—We do not join the church because we are perfect, but because it is a chief means which God has provided for our growth in grace. We do not attend school because we are fine scholars, but because we wish to be. The unconverted should not be asked, first of all, to "join the church," but to "come to Christ." To ask them to join the church before they are interested in their own salvation, would be either meaningless to them or excite their opposition. Only those believed to be already Christians should be asked to unite with the church.

Coming into the church is not crossing a line drawn in the sand, but stepping up to a higher plane; and all should be taught that joining the church imposes obligation, and that loyalty is demanded. Those who hesitate to unite with the church because of morbid conceptions of the obligations involved should be encouraged by a presentation of the spiritual benefits to be derived. The first step in conversion is necessarily not a public one. The first step should be to confess in the heart to God, and this will prepare for the public avowal. True, these actions may be simultaneous.

(5). Answering Objections. It will be impossible, in the space at command, to do more than offer a few suggestions on this important subject.

(a). How to Deal with a Caviller or Moralist.

Give him a direct answer from Scripture.

Keep him to the point of the argument.

Bring him face to face with the sin question.

"Answer a fool according to his folly."

"Answer not a fool according to his folly."

Which to do depends on the kind of fool he is and the nature of his folly.

Be collected and let him get excited.

Put him on the defensive.

Let him entangle himself, and then bring him face to face with his contradictions.

Get a common ground to stand on, and then apply the *argumentum ad hominem;* that is, show that his argument is inconststent with his position. This was a common method with Christ.

Make him answer his own questions.

Be able to give personal experience testifying to the power of the truth you proclaim.

A gentleman said that he did not belong to the church, though he supported the gospel, and that "actions speak louder than words." The reply was, "Yes, and your action in not identifying yourself with the people of God speaks louder than all your professions about helping the church."

On one occasion an arguer declared that we could never banish the saloon from our country, and afterward inadvertently remarked that he believed in the "survival of the fittest." The reply was: "And so do I; and unless you can prove that a saloon is fitter to exist than a Christian church, you must admit that the saloon will have to go. That is an end of argument." And so it was; he could not rally with a retort.

(*b*). How to Deal with a Doubter.

To convince doubters, we must be believers, and believe with all our might.

We must be able to give reasons for the faith within us, and be patient in explaining the truth to a doubter. Do not dismiss the subject lazily. If you have passed through experiences of doubt, show how you were led into the light.

When doubt is the child of neglect, get the doubter to take up neglected duties.

Make much use of God's Word,

(*c*). An Incorrigible Person.

Be as incorrigible as he is. A continual dropping will wear away a stone.

Pray for him and for yourself.

Sometimes you should give up specific effort for this or that person, for it is required that we should not "cast pearls before swine" or waste useful strength; but in this we need divine direction to know our duty.

(*d*). The Faultfinder.

To the oft-repeated statement that there are "hypocrites in the church," different replies are possible, such as,—

"Are there any hypocrites in your business?"

"Plenty of them."

"Then why are you in it?"

Or, "Was your mother a member of the church?"

"Yes."

"Was she a hypocrite?"

"Certainly not!"

"Then that proves that there is such a thing as true religion, and if so, you ought to strive to possess it."

Or, "Do people counterfeit notes of a good or of a worthless bank?"

"Only of the good bank."

"Then counterfeit Christians prove the reality of Christianity."

(*e*). The honest inquirer should be patiently instructed.

The following questions and answers will illustrate.

"I do not feel that I am a great sinner."

Ans. Nicodemus was not a great sinner, in the eyes of the world, but a good man; yet he needed to be born again. John 3: 3, 5, 7.

"How do I know that Jesus means me by the invitation?"

Ans. He died for all who will come. John 6:37; Isa. 55:1.

"How can God give salvation just for the accepting?"

Ans. Because of his love. John 3:16.

"I do not feel that I am saved."

Ans. The Bible does not say, "Feel and be saved," but "Believe and be saved." Feeling is a result of believing. Acts 16:31.

"Is there anything besides just believing?"

Ans. Yes; repent and confess. 2 Cor. 7:10; Rom. 10:9, 10.

"I have not knowledge enough to be a Christian; I do not understand the Bible."

Ans. You know enough to be saved, and God will teach you to serve. Isa. 35:8; John 16:13.

"I will come by and by."

Ans. There is no promise for to-morrow. Heb. 4:7; 2 Cor. 6:2.

"How long must I continue to seek?"

Ans. In one sense no time at all, for God has been seeking you. Luke 19:10. In the sense of grasping his promise, you will have to seek only till you are able to put all your heart into it. Jer. 29:13; 2 Cor. 6:2.

"I am too great a sinner to be saved."

Ans. God says the contrary. Isa. 1:18.

"I am afraid the day of salvation for me is past."

Ans. That is one of Satan's lies to keep you away from Christ. Heb. 4:7; 2 Cor. 6:2.

"I am afraid I cannot remain faithful."

Ans. In your present state you have no power, but if you come, God will give you daily grace. You must avail yourself of the privileges, and you will obtain the promises. John 15; 2 Cor. 9:8; 2 Pet. 3:18; Gal. 6:9; Heb. 2:1; 10:24, 25; Rom. 5:10; 8, and many other passages.

"How may I know I am saved?"

Ans. Through God's Word. Rom. 5:1–5; 8:16; John 6:37; 2 Cor. 5:17; 1 John 3:14; 5:2, 10, 11.

"I can be as good a Christian and do as much good outside the church as in it."

Ans. That contradicts God's wisdom in establishing the church. A professed Christian outside the church does as much harm as a hypocrite inside, leading others astray. Acts 2:47; Mark 8:38.

Teach the inquirer to study for himself, to pray, to keep his mind fixed on the great subject of his salvation, to follow diligently any ray of light he may have. Assist him with your own experience and with facts from the experience of others. Let the work be thorough, but remember that there may be varieties of experience, all genuine.

(6). Work in the House of God. If we brought to Christ only the unconverted persons who come to the services of the Lord's house, the church would have a continual revival. How important, then, that Christians should seek for skill and cultivate carefulness in speaking to strangers ! For this purpose, workers should not all occupy front seats at church and Endeavor meetings, but some should post themselves in the rear of the room, that they may look after the needs of visitors and be able to speak to them at the close of the service in a natural way. Here the social, lookout, and prayer-meeting committees, and indeed all Christians, should find a field for activity in ascertaining as many facts about strangers as the time will allow,— their residence and church affiliations, if any, to use in future work; but especially should they greet them kindly and introduce them to other members of the church.

(7). *Getting Young Men to Church.*—We must believe in the power of invitation. If young men were invited more frequently, they would attend in larger numbers. Then they must not be overlooked when present. Adult males in the church must be active in this department. Men must work with men. The character of the service has much to do with the matter. Some theorists say that young men want sermons that are "up to the times" and that stimulate mental activity. The judgment of the author is, that young men want the plain gospel preached from the heart and backed up by a high grade of Christian living in the church. To catch young men, we must not lower our standard, but raise it. The gospel does not need to be apologized for or concealed from immortal minds to win their love. Faithful work and faithful prayer will succeed. Some will resist the Spirit of God, but when they do, workers should not find fault with and reject the pure gospel for some device judged to be more "fetching." In adapting truth do not substitute error. A small congregation carrying the truth home in their hearts will be more active in Christian work than a large congregation unconvicted.

5. *Assisting the New Convert.*—Many dangers menace the new convert, and the Christian worker must continue his fostering care, pointing out the errors into which one may fall, and also the sources of strength, giving frankly of his own heart's experience of struggle and triumph, that the other may avoid failure, and obtain strength.

(1). One of the temptations of the young convert is to relax the earnestness shown during the period of his conviction, trusting to the feeling of security he has attained. He should be taught to press forward with at least as much vigor as he showed in coming to the cross. When Satan finds a Christian off his guard, he springs up with a sudden temptation.

(2). Christians often neglect the new convert, believing him safe, and many church-members are not themselves in training to assist the beginner along the heavenward road.

(3). The new convert, as a rule, does not let his struggles be known, thinking it a kind of reflection on himself to acknowledge that he is not in the same state of blessing as formerly; but he should seek instant help from God and also from Christian brethren.

(4). When feeling subsides, the young Christian may think he never was saved, and give up ·in despair. Some, indeed, may not have accepted Christ truly, but an honest confession at this point and nurture by Christians would lead to Christ.

(5). A convert's heart is like a newly planted garden; the weeds appearing quickly must instantly be plucked up and the good plants tended.

(6). Self-trust should never be permitted. The motto should be, "Trusting . . . I strive."

(7). Older Christians should pray for the young converts and help them in every way by counsel and by encouragement.

(8). Young converts may help one another by an interchange of confidences. Having similar needs, they will understand one another, and the help one receives may be passed to the rest.

6. *Training Converts for Service.*—One reason why there are so many weaklings in the church is because Christians frequently cease effort for the advancement of those newly converted. How large is the number of cases of "arrested development"!

No worker does his duty well who designs merely to save people from death. He should have for his ideal the training of those persons for service also. Thus he multiplies himself. It is our duty to increase the number of workers, because it is our duty to use methods that will result in the saving of the largest number of souls; hence, every Christian must become a teacher. By this process the worker will grow constantly in grace, and the other will develop into a worker. He who thus keeps in mind the ever-recurring needs of souls out of Christ, and of souls that have come to Christ, will have no time or inclination for participation in the follies of the world.

(1). One method of training is by workers' Bible training-classes. This method consists, first, of a study of the Bible as a text-book, to learn to analyze the Scriptures and to acquire their methods; and, second, of discussions of plans, of difficulties encountered and successes attained, based on reports of work done by the members of the class. It also includes comprehensive instruction in church-work in general, personal service, the leading of meetings, the teaching of classes, etc.

(2). The points included in this chapter are intended for the instruction of older Christians that they may win souls, then for the instruction of the souls that are won. The worker can take the new convert over the ground he has himself traversed.

7. *Last, in order to emphasize its supreme importance, the reception of the Holy Spirit*, to equip for service and life, is emphasized. No worker is properly trained who does not have this blessing, no new convert properly led who does not seek this enduement.

How to receive the Spirit is a matter for earnest contemplation.

(1). Every one should remember the Father's declaration of his willingness to bestow the Holy Spirit, not upon some Christians, but upon all; he is more willing than earthly parents are to give good gifts to their children. We receive the Spirit as we receive salvation—by faith.

(2). There should be a study of the Spirit's work; to endeavor to understand what he comes to do reveals more fully human need.

(3). The lives of spiritual persons should be studied; from their biographies we may learn how they came into the possession of such power; and conversation with those who have the manifestation of the Spirit may furnish like instruction.

(4). Self-surrender puts us into the frame for receiving the Spirit. God sends his power through the soul that is ready to be used, as men turn the current of a river through a water-wheel prepared for the purpose. The ten days' waiting before Pentecost was not simply for the purpose of prayer, but was a test of self-surrender and of determination to leave the world and follow the teachings of Jesus the crucified; they who stayed the ten days thus evidenced the fact that their minds were wholly fixed on the new service.

(5). Pentecost was only the beginning of blessing. It was the induction into a spiritual life, but did not fit at once for every future need. As some one has said, it was the "peep of day." When the communion of power is opened, the Christian is to continue to commune and to receive the teachings of the Holy Spirit. For lack of appreciation of this truth, many fail to grow in spiritual power, thinking their past experience sufficient and conclusive.

(6). We often pray for a "pouring out" of the Spirit, when we should rather pray for his "manifestation," admitting the fact of his presence and our blindness.

(7). All the foregoing has nothing to do with the reception of the Holy Spirit by every Christian when he comes to Christ, nor with the preceding work of the Spirit by which souls are saved, but refers to that larger measure of power which Christians may obtain and which so many professedly lack.

III. Open-Air Work.

The author assisted in open-air work, on street corners and elsewhere, for some four years, and out of this experience commends this line of service as most feasible and important. It should be a natural outgrowth of Christian Endeavor energy. While more courage is necessary here than almost anywhere else, yet with experience it will seem but little, if any, harder than other lines of service. Besides, how necessary is this work, corresponding to that of the hedges and lanes spoken of in the Saviour's parables!

1. *To organize the work.*

(1). Do not seek to get united action on the part of the community before beginning. Let a few start somewhere, and enlarge the work.

(2). If you organize fully, let there be a president, superintendent or executive officer, secretary, treasurer, and devotional committee (of which the superintendent is one), to appoint meetings, secure leaders, and arrange the relays of workers. All these officers should constitute an executive committee.

(3). Occasionally have workers' meetings, to hear reports from the field, to pray, and to talk over plans.

(4). Keep a list of members, and send them postal-card announcements of such meetings. Workers should try to bring others, to interest them.

(5). Let each member see that the work is announced in his church, mentioned in prayer meeting, etc., that the congregation may become interested. A great good will be done if churches simply have the work in mind.

(6). Several simultaneous meetings may be held each Lord's Day evening in various parts of the city or town, at such hours as experience may show best suited for the purpose, and also on other evenings of the week.

(7). These meetings should consist of the usual gospel services, followed with distribution of leaflets, and with personal conversation with inquirers, where possible.

(8). The plan of meeting should be arranged previous to the gathering, so that each one will know what he is to do. Some may be able to do nothing at first but help to sing, but they will gain strength as the meetings proceed. One may be assigned to lead the singing; another to have charge of the distribution of reading-matter; another to count the audiences, note the general character of the meeting, and make report on the same.

2. *In conducting the meetings*

(1). Begin with singing. Continue until a crowd has gathered.

(2). Read a Scripture lesson (as a rule, this should be brief), and follow with prayer.

(3). In remarks, use plenty of Scripture quotations, for the most part giving chapter and verse.

Some in the audience may remember where the text is to be found, and afterward look it up for themselves.

(4). What is said should be simple, direct, and practical. Wherever your own experience has proved the truth of your statements, let the fact be known. Incidents drawn from your own observation will help to interest and convince.

(5). At times, it will be better to have three or four short talks instead of one long one.

(6). If you are a layman, say so; it may establish a bond of sympathy between you and your hearers.

(7). Prayer may be introduced at the close of the remarks.

(8). Do not protract the service.

(9). If you expect to hold other meetings, state the fact, and announce where they will be held. Also announce meetings by placards and through the newspapers.

(10). Workers should distribute themselves through the audience, so as to come in contact with the interested and impenitent.

(11). It is a good plan to take some unconverted person to the meeting, and after service walk back with him and follow up the impressions made.

(12). In distributing literature, be careful to speak of it as "leaflets," not as "tracts." It is well to let your remarks be often along the line of the literature you intend to distribute. Refer, if you can, to something in the leaflet, and say at the close that you will distribute to any who may wish to read more fully,

(13). Announce where you may be found during the week, that persons who may wish may write or call upon you.

(14). Be patient and kind under interruption and annoyance, and pray for God's grace before, during, and after each service.

(15). At times, buildings in process of erection can be secured for services, by taking proper precautions against accident and fire.

(16). After-services are possible, in certain instances, to be held in private houses near at hand.

(17.) Tent meetings may be held with good results.

(18). In closing a season of open-air work, make an effort to have the last meeting the largest and best of all, and distribute souvenir cards containing Scripture texts and announcements of the names and locations of churches.

IV. Rescue Mission Work.

The suggestions under this head are the result of the author's experience in connection with an industrial mission, but, so far as the holding of services is concerned, will be useful in any mission.

1. *Industrial missions* should be founded in all cities of size. Many of the schemes for assisting the poor in our cities might be appropriately named "Associations for the Promotion of Pauperism," since they train people to depend on charity, to the injury of their own energy and self-respect. The industrial mission provides for the issuance of rations, fuel, or clothing, in return

for work done. It enables the worthy poor to maintain themselves during periods of great scarcity, and ministers to their mental, moral, and spiritual advancement. It provides for a mitigation of the tramp nuisance through a system of tickets, issued by patrons of the mission, entitling the recipient to the privilege of laboring for lodging, including a compulsory bath, or food, thus guarding against imposture. The limits of this book preclude more than this general indorsement of the plan and plea for its promotion.

2. *For the gospel meetings*, a four-page leaflet should be prepared, on the first page of which such information as the following should be printed.

The devotional committee consists of seven members, one member to have special care for the music at the services, and the other six to take weekly turns in conducting the meetings. Sabbath services will be conducted by the superintendent.

The leader appointed for any week will be responsible for the conduct of the services each night, either by leading or procuring leaders; so far as possible, the leader for the week should attend every one of the services for which he is responsible. He should follow the suggestions of this leaflet in conducting the meetings and following up results.

The weekly leader may divide the duties enumerated for each evening with several persons. The usual time for an entire service should be about an hour. Controversy must be strictly prohibited.

The programme will be: (*a*) An opening song service for ten or fifteen minutes. (*b*) Scripture reading, prayer, and remarks, varied as occasion may require. (*c*) Testimony by Christians present. This must be kept well in hand and discreetly managed, and may be omitted altogether, if deemed advisable. (*d*) Invitations to the unconverted. The person in charge should see to it that there are a sufficient number of workers to speak personally with inquirers, especially at the close of the service. These workers should be distributed through the audience. An "inquiry meeting" may sometimes be held.

The name and address of each inquirer should be obtained, together with his church preference, if he has any, and recorded on the blank provided in this leaflet for that purpose. If the individual professes conversion, the letter C should be placed after his name. Any other helpful information may be recorded, and at the end of the week the record left on file in the office of the association. The leader should keep a copy for his own use. Each night, also, the names of inquirers should be filed in the office.

Each weekly leader is expected to follow up the persons who have shown an interest in salvation, and endeavor to complete the work begun. It may not always be possible to make personal visits. Final information as to results is to be placed on file in the association office.

A tally of attendance should be kept each night on the blank provided.

An effort should be made to give personal greetings to all who attend.

Monday night of each week is to be kept as "young people's night," and the weekly leaders are asked to arrange with young people's societies for workers for such nights.

One night of each week may be reserved for popular lectures. In such cases, a brief devotional service is to be held immediately before or after the lecture, as may be deemed advisable by the superintendent.

It is understood that the superintendent has the right to preserve order in the meetings, and to act as an executive officer when necessary.

Meetings of this committee for conference will be held from time to time, at the call of the chairman.

On pages two and three of the leaflet there should be blanks for each day, to record results, such as the following.

Monday............................. 18 .
LEADER.....................................
Tally of attendance............; Total.......
Names of inquirers, etc.........................

Page four should contain the names and addresses of the members of the devotional committee.

V. Rewards of Service.

Many are deterred from activity in Christian work because of a false impression concerning its difficulties and the self-denial required; but it should be remembered that we have been looking over the whole field, and that the duties are not so crowded as the general outlook would indicate. Tasks come one by one, with grace for each. If we were to look over the whole field of blessing as we have over the field of service, we should find the mingled prospect of grace and duty most attractive. Consecration takes away the excrescences and the controlling power of sin; experience extracts the roots and refines the nature till it is fit for the highest service.

To a young Christian who maintained her principles in the face of great opposition, and who frequently appealed to another for advice and comfort, this reply, in substance, was sent, expressing certain truths that apply widely: "Your letters enable me to do personal work in helping you, and thus I am better equipped for service in the general work of the Lord. I am encouraged by the knowledge that there is real heroism in the world, as exemplified in your case; your faithfulness inspires me to better endeavors, and gives me facts with which to encourage others; and you thus turn your suffering to practical account in doing the work of the Lord through me. Such an experience as yours will draw you nearer God, and you should not complain of that which enables you to come closer to him."

The worker always helps himself when he helps others; even the cases that are long continued have their own particular value—they supply the need for difficult lessons, and furnish the means of creating a good fibre in our experience. They are an understudy for him who would be not a mere novice, but an artist, in the work of the gospel.

The routine of every-day service is like the rising and setting of the sun that brings the changing centuries. Such plodding forces furnish the basis for all that is grand and useful in nature. There is not much variety in the turning of a wheel on its axle, but the circumference of the wheel has variety enough as it rolls on over hills and through vales; so, while there must always be something about our service in the nature of restriction, mechanical exactness, and painful repetition, yet thereby the circumference of our lives is made to touch at every point, in a series of experiences never twice alike, the wide diversity of nature.

We are better examples to our brethren when we exhibit the skill that comes of patient training, possible to all, than when we display a marvellous gift impossible to the many. If a Christian intends to give self-denying service, he might as well continue the work in which he finds himself engaged as seek the same kind of service elsewhere.

It has been said that a Christian should have a restful centre and that centre is Jesus Christ. But it is also true that a Christian must have a sphere of constant activity, for a restful centre is like the axis of the earth, and is the only thing that is at rest. Trust in God is the axis for our sphere of striving. The peace of God is the point around which our service of God revolves.

PART V.—SUPPLEMENTARY.

CHAPTER I.

QUESTION-BOX.

Under this head are gathered certain points omitted from the body of the book, or rather set apart from it, to emphasize the query department as an element in Christian work and as a sample of the proper method of answering questions.

How to answer and how not to answer questions needs specific, though brief, attention. The answer should be direct, not roundabout; simple, not involved; clear, not obscure; and should present a high standard, not a low one. It should not enter into other subjects that might be suggested by it; as, for instance, if one should ask whether it is proper to go swimming on the Lord's Day, and the answer should include a discussion of taking a bath in the home—a case within the author's knowledge. Answer the question that is asked; leave others until they are asked.

1. *What can affiliated members do for the society?*

They can work in a truly Endeavor-like way for the mid-week prayer meeting, and secure the promise of persons to attend, or to attend and participate.

2. *Is there any way to read a statistical report so as to make it interesting?*

I once heard this done to perfection by Mrs. W. B. Besserer, of Middleport, O., the secretary of an Endeavor union. In going over the various items after the name of each society, she read all that was encouraging in a bright, clear voice, and all that was otherwise in a much lower tone, with a significant inflection, and perhaps accompanied with a slight deprecatory shake of the head. It was most interesting and effective.

3. *If the pastor is not interested in our Endeavor work, how can we interest him?*

Volunteer to help him in his work; go to him for counsel; send him to the conventions.

4. *What do you think of the Brotherhood of Andrew and Philip?*

That it is a good organization, and that its methods could be applied to the Christian Endeavor society by the appointment of a "Brotherhood committee."

5. *Would you advise Intermediate societies of Christian Endeavor?*

Only in large churches where the Endeavorers are too numerous to participate in the Young People's and Junior societies. I would not have Intermediate societies just for the purpose of fixing a new grade.

6. *You insist on persons' giving the results of their experiments and avoiding theories. Do you not think much good has come from theorizing?*

Yes; but first try your theories in your own field. A worker is not always theorizing when he recommends a new adaptation of a plan, for his experience *practically* covers the point proposed, though he has not *specifically* attempted it. A theorist spins fancies out of his brain, to be demonstrated later. An absolutely logical deduction from a proved fact is not a theory, but a corollary.

7. *Should a worker cease his efforts when it is apparent that he is accomplishing nothing?*

That depends on whether some one else could take his place and accomplish more, and whether there is anything else for the worker to do.

8. *How shall we raise money for Endeavor society expenses?*

By individual pledges and offerings once a month.

9. *If a leader is known to be a blunderer, would you continue to ask him to lead?*

Yes, if he blundered along the right road.

I once heard a leader who made many blunders in reading the Scripture lesson; he called "antiChrist" "anarchist,"—not a bad interpretation,— and made other mistakes. Noticing his errors, and fearing the result, I prayed that God would bless the meeting in spite of the mistakes, or use the mistakes to his glory; and after the leader had finished the reading, he made most excellent remarks, and the meeting turned out to be the very best for some weeks. This shows how we may, by prayer, get a blessing that shall obliterate the memory of antecedent blunders, encourage our hearts with a demonstration of God's power, and show that honest efforts in his strength will produce rich results.

10. *Is it not a good plan to have persons pledge*

themselves to pray during the entire prayer-meeting hour for the manifestation of God's Spirit?

No, for that might mean that they did not expect the Spirit to manifest himself till the close of the meeting. Let people pray till they feel that their prayers are answered.

11. *What can be done to create continued interest in the monthly meetings of local-union executive committees?*

Aside from the regular reports, give special attention to some one line of work each month. Announce this special topic a month in advance. If some line has been neglected, take up that, or bring in new features for consideration. Also have a question-box on society methods frequently. Make the meetings useful in an "all-round" way.

12. *Ought there to be Junior unions in cities and towns?*

There should be meetings of Junior superintendents for the discussion of their work, and also rallies for the Juniors. If a Junior union is formed, it should not be officered by Juniors, but by the superintendents. The Junior work can be conducted successfully as a department of the local union, by the appointment of a local-union Junior superintendent, who should report at the executive-committee meetings like any other chairman. Once in two months the Junior work might be a special topic in the executive-committee meeting, thus bringing this line of effort specifically to the attention of the young people's societies. In any case, pains should be taken to keep the Juniors and young people in close fellowship. No plans should be adopted that would break up the Endeavor work of any locality into fragments.

13. *What would you do if unsuccessful in a work?*

Undertake another; success there might bring the old work to a successful issue.

14. *Is the study of the Old Testament necessary to the equipment of a Christian worker?*

Is the ability to paint a background necessary to the equipment of an artist?

15. *Is it proper to accept for church-work money that has been made dishonestly?*

Is it proper for a church to be a receiver of stolen goods?

16. *Is it not true that a good many young people go to Christian Endeavor meetings just to meet one another?*

Is it not true that that is a good place to meet?

17. *Is it consistent to do Christian work while one is conscious of great shortcomings in himself?*

Is it consistent to do good, and thus grow in grace?

18. *Would you discuss religious questions in a crowd of unbelievers and cavillers?*

The Saviour often did. Study his method, and follow it. If you can silence a caviller, you will do a good thing. Do not discuss merely for discussion's sake, but a Christian should be able to maintain his cause so as not to let evil men gain an advantage.

19. *Why are the interiors of many churches so imperfectly adapted to the use intended?*

The outside was first planned, and the inside suffered in consequence. The order should be reversed. It would not prevent tasty exteriors.

20. *In what way is the Christian Endeavor society a part of the church, as stated in the constitution?*

Most of its active members are members of the church; it exists for Christ and the church; and each individual society is under the authority of the church or congregation where it exists.

21. *Is it really possible to get a large attendance of young men at the Christian Endeavor meetings?*

My own society for months has averaged almost exactly as many males as females. When the attendance was much smaller than now, the ratio was about the same, and the increase, therefore, has been about the same for one sex as the other.

22. *Is there not danger that one may become narrow in opposing all methods of church-work that are not up to the strictly religious standard?*

The bore of a cannon is not too small if the ball fits it. The church is the cannon, the gospel is the ball, and should fill the circumference of the bore absolutely. The "rifles," or grooves, in the ordnance are not for worldly padding, but are the consecrations of the members, imparting directness to the projectile and promoting the cleanliness of the barrel. The power (*dunamis*) of the Spirit is the powder. The effectiveness of the shot would not be promoted, but hindered, by foreign substances in the barrel.

23. *What is the meaning of the word "Bible"?*

It comes from a Greek word, *biblos*, signifying a book. The Bible is emphatically the Book.

24. *Is the world growing better or worse?*

Well, would you rather live now or eighteen hundred years ago?

25. *At the monthly consecration meeting, should the names of the associate members be given with the active at the roll-call?*

The associate members are not expected to take part in the consecration meeting; such participation would be meaningless for persons not Christians. If the associate roll is called, the associates should be expected to do no more than answer "Present"; and as they have promised to attend the meetings, I see no objection to calling the roll, to impress upon them their obligation in this regard. But the associate list should be called separately.

26. *If I do not know that a certain action is wrong, may I not perform it?*

It is not sufficient that you do not know it to be wrong, you must know that it is right. "Whatsoever is not of faith is sin."

CHAPTER II.

PROVERBS AND SEED THOUGHTS.

[Besides the use of these condensed truths as aids to reflection, they illustrate the value of epigrammatic utterances in Christian Endeavor meetings. It is good discipline and good service to reduce a whole speech to a suggestive sentence.]

"A holy life speaks all languages."
Fully ready means joyful performance.
He who possesses true grace has the real graces.
Short preparation makes long process.
Self-indulgence rots the soul.
Obedience is resignation grown active.
Tardy obedience makes timid performance.
A lagging step makes a cowardly heart.
An excuse is first cousin to a falsehood.
Reasons exist; excuses have to be made.
A general promise includes the details.
We must sow action to reap feeling.
An excuse-maker is a promise-breaker.
A worker is blessed if his work is blessed.
It is not work, but worry, that kills.
We cannot expect position without opposition.
To be faithful, one must be full of faith.
Enthusiasm is not noise, but persistence.
Some are called stubborn, who are only intense.
The soul that is self-centred has no horizon.
When one beholds Christ, he prays for his enemies.

"Didn't Think" is a full brother to "Don't Care."

Self-mastery is always preceded by self-surrender.

God will take care of those who let God use them.

A man's duty is his best opportunity.

Humility and thanksgiving dwell together in the heart, when united with the bond of faith.

An "up-to-date" Christian is an all-round Christian.

If you cannot be an Esther before the king, be a Mordecai in the gate.

He fears no consequences who believes in principles.

Sectarianism is composed of superstition and selfishness, equal parts.

People who want to "hold out" should hold on.

The nettle difficulty will not sting the hand resolution.

Consecration is to the soul what concentration is to the mind.

The backslider soon begins to wonder if he is not a hypocrite.

A promise once easy becomes difficult if neglected.

When truth takes possession of a man, it makes him aggressive.

We have no more right to waste our thoughts than our time.

A young man's glory is his strength, but his grace is in his trust.

One cannot be true to himself unless he is true to God's plan concerning him.

Grudging service and grudging giving are alike to be condemned.

We must not get tired putting time into a work that is to stand for eternity.

We learn by imitation and repetition, by analysis and synthesis.

A spiritual vacuum feels all outside duties as a burden.

That is not a good conscience which does not lead to self-denial.

The purest love always seeks the highest good.

Self-denial is the spinal column of consistency.

The ambition of a Christian should not be to perform a brave act, but to lead a brave life.

We gain knowledge by studying that which we do not understand, and courage by undertaking that which frightens us.

The aim of the minister should be not so much to preach fine sermons as to proclaim fine truth.

No one is an honest doubter unless he is an honest investigator.

To be artists in expression, we must be chemists in thought.

We can carry the world on our hearts, but we cannot carry it on our shoulders.

Doing the next duty always leads to further light on the path.

This age is a time for greatness of soul, not for weakness of principle.

There is a vast difference between thinking and nursing an opinion.

The faithful preaching of fundamentals leads to the careful performance of details.

One way to have good meetings is, to do good between meetings.

Remembering slights will prevent recalling delights.

We should cultivate the flowers as well as pull up the weeds.

By feeding on the promises we get strength to obey the commands.

Real tact is full sister to humility, and distrusts herself.

To plan wisely is as much a duty as to labor earnestly.

We should confess our joys as well as our trials.

In Christian work, we do not need æsthetes, but athletes.

No system in the work can be successful without system in the worker.

We should be "poor in spirit," but not poor-spirited.

No one is independent of that which is below him until he is dependent on that which is above him.

A "workman that needeth not to be ashamed" "studies to show himself approved."

A good many difficulties in churches are best "settled" by being ignored.

Studying the fulfilment of the prophecies gives faith to believe the promises.

We are responsible for all the good we might have done and for all the harm we might have prevented.

It has been said that riding a hobby is like riding a hobby-horse; there is a great deal of motion, but no progress.

One should recognize his abilities, that he may feel his responsibilities.

Too many churches and societies are afflicted with "dead wood" on the one side and dead works on the other.

We do not truly keep our Christian Endeavor pledge unless we try to help others keep their pledge.

We should not give currency to our doubts, but only to our convictions.

Our feelings rise into the realm of true poetry when we receive divine blessing. All joy is melodious.

We get knowledge by listening to things we do not understand, and acquire courage by attempting that which frightens us.

Victories won create a thirst for more victories; thus conflict becomes a nursery of happiness.

When retiring from a duty, we walk in its shadow; when going ahead to its performance, we walk in its light.

You can win by means of *pluck*, but if you do not " mind your p's," you'll have to trust to *luck*.

Some think they are patiently hoping, when they are only indolently waiting.

If we go no faster than the crowd, we cannot flatter ourselves that we are of value as leaders.

It is well at times to win banners for ourselves, but it is always well to pluck others' standards out of the mire.

God's call to us may come through a friend, and he may also send us to call others.

When we go to the front, it should be to impel

others to increased activity; and when we retire to the rear, it should be to help the stragglers.

The "preaching demanded by the times" is just the preaching demanded by perishing souls.

It is far-reaching purpose that makes zeal continuous.

Strength unexpended on some worthy object turns and devours its possessor.

Some rude plans would be most efficacious, if refined. Many useful ideas fail for lack of a little polishing.

Good methods have been "born to blush unseen" for lack of a little care in describing their merits to others.

We learn by imitation and repetition; hence the value of good examples in our lives and reviews in our studies.

The flame of consecration is kindled from on high, but we must keep the altar supplied with fuel.

"It is a long lane that has no turning." But we need desire no turning, if the lane leads where we wish to go. We should not be weary in well-doing.

When one can find nothing else to do, that is a good time to clean around his own door-step.

It takes a reverent mind to find true happiness. Discipline is required to extract joy from outward circumstances, or to recognize real pleasure at sight.

"Trusting" and "I promise" walk hand in hand through every difficulty and danger.

Christian joy is not shown by a stereotyped

smile, but by taking up duties with gladness of heart, and by communicating the hopeful spirit to others.

"The next step after obliterating the line between the world and the church will be to obliterate the church."—(Clark Waggoner.)

To mourn over that for which we are not responsible prevents seeing the duties for which we are responsible.

Between failing to do things that look too simple to be of consequence and those that seem too hard to be accomplished, many people manage to get nothing done.

The disciples who would fish for men must often endure the storms of life's Galilee.

Zeal is not confined to the performance of outward duties, but is exhibited in private study and devotion.

There is one position always open to the would-be worker, and that is, to become the "servant of all."

Having faith, we get knowledge, by first adding virtue (that is, "vigor" or "courage"), and attempting something for God.

Confession is just the bubbling over of faith; and the study of the Word brings faith.

The word "Spirit" means "breath"; and when the Holy Spirit is manifested in a church, there is a spiritual atmosphere that woos men and women to the gospel. We should seek to promote such an atmosphere by doing none but spiritual things.

Sinners will not trust themselves to a wabbly Christian any more than they will to a shaky bridge.

If you cannot do anything but odds and ends, be an expert in odds and ends. In " little things be great."

To wear a C. E. pin leads others to Constant Expectation of good deeds from the wearer.

Innocence that remains only innocent becomes sinful. The measure of duty is not fulfilled by being only harmless.

A Christian is a "straight-edge," to be used in bringing things to a right standard, and should not try to make himself adjustable to the crookedness of the world.

"How would the Lord like me to spend this money?" is quite as much a question for the Endeavorer as "What would the Lord like to have me do?"

We should be steadfast in our work, not merely because we have promised, but because God has promised.

What we hear may nourish our thought when the form of words is forgotten, as the rain sunk from sight may promote chemical change in the plant.

"It is said that a new broom sweeps clean, but it takes an old broom to get into corners."—(Miss I. Martin.)

"The trouble with many persons' prayers is, that they have too many words, and too few wants."—(O. M. Sala.)

We do not get God's approval until we have done something to warrant it. If you want the sweets of hearing God call you wise, you must first hear the world call you a fool.

We can prepare for soul-saving by holding to all

the truth we have and compromising none of it away. Stand fast is the way to win.

Both ruts and rails mark definite lines, but rails are laid by progress and ruts are worn by custom —the difference between real activity and stolid indifference.

God sometimes leads us along a pathway of service, not because we are to follow it forever, but to bring us to a point of view from which we may see another line of duty that would otherwise have been hidden.

Tramps are disagreeable from disuse of soap and water. What shall we say of the Christian who neglects spiritual cleansing and does not seek purification from daily defilement ?

All learning, all philosophy, and all experience should be shod with the iron point of practical application. Note the personal element in the character of Paul's work as shown in the last chapter of Romans.

There is a crown of glory for youth as well as age. The laurels of a conqueror may be won by triumph over early temptations as well as by victories over the sins of mature years.

Conscience is not a moral guide, but a moral restraint. It is a red flag to mark unsafe places, but not all places are safe where the flag is unseen.

"I forgot" is no excuse for the non-performance of duty, unless there is an excuse for forgetting. From forgetting duty it is not a long road to forgetting God.

"I had no time" is no excuse for him who wastes time or prefers selfishness to service.

In the race of life the devil has a start of every

secret disciple, of every one who is master of his own actions and yet will not confess.

Young life is an uncut diamond. It should be cut and polished, till from innumerable facets it reflects the light of heaven. It is a telescope, as yet unfocused, that needs to be adjusted to behold the wonders of different universes.

To cite cases of Christians who follow popular amusements and yet keep up their church-work, is no more a commendation of those amusements than it would be a commendation of intoxicants to cite the case of a moderate drinker who still supported his family.

A bad man is like a dirty liquid, which, if allowed to settle, becomes clear on top but foul at the bottom. A Christian is like a medicine that must be shaken before using. Stir up a bad man, and you get sediment; stir up a good man, and you get sentiment. Truth proclaimed exposes the vile on the one hand and arouses true Christianity on the other.

A Christian face is not always a smiling one; it is a mirror of the soul, and reflects joy, sympathy, seriousness, and abhorrence of sin.

A young person should be led to a high purpose simultaneously with his first conception of his powers and possibilities; otherwise he may spend his strength in empty rejoicings, and answer for this waste to God. (Prov. 20:29; Eccl. 11:9).

The soldier who really loves his cause is delighted with the mere approval of his commander. So the Christian worker will find sweet reward when the heavenly Father says, "Well done, good and faithful servant!"

The Temple Series.

Dainty cloth bindings. Illustrated.

Price, 35 cents each, postpaid.

United Society of Christian Endeavor,
Boston and Chicago.